CLASSICAL COMICS STUDY GUIDE

Making the classics accessible
for teachers and students

Suitable for teaching ages 10–17

Written by: Gavin Knight

THE GRAPHIC NOVEL
Charles Dickens

CLASSICAL COMICS STUDY GUIDE

Great Expectations: The Graphic Novel

First UK Edition

Published by: Classical Comics Ltd

Written by: Gavin Knight
Additional information by: Ian McNeilly

Character Designs and Original Artwork: John Stokes
Design & Layout: Jo Wheeler, Jenny Placentino & Carl Andrews

Editor in Chief: Clive Bryant

The rights of Gavin Knight, Ian McNeilly and John Stokes to be
identified as the authors and artists of this work have been
asserted in accordance with the Copyright, Designs and Patents
Act 1988 sections 77 and 78.

Acknowledgments: Every effort has been made to trace
copyright holders of material reproduced in this book. Any rights
not acknowledged here will be acknowledged in subsequent
editions if notice is given to Classical Comics Ltd.

All enquiries should be addressed to:
Classical Comics Ltd.
PO Box 7280
Litchborough
Towcester
NN12 9AR
United Kingdom
Tel: 0845 812 3000

education@classicalcomics.com
www.classicalcomics.com

ISBN: 978-1-906332-13-6

Printed in the UK

CONTENTS

INTRODUCTION

WELCOME TO THE *GREAT EXPECTATIONS* STUDY GUIDE FROM CLASSICAL COMICS.

I write the introduction to this study guide on a shingle beach looking out towards the Isle of Sheppey. Charles Dickens lived there as a small boy. All of his life he loved this coastline; the beaches, the people, the dreamy nature of days like today when life seems easier, colours seem brighter, and inspiration catches fire.

Not so long ago twenty million Britons tuned in to the *I'd Do Anything* final, a television show whose purpose was to choose the nation's favourite "Nancy". Telephone lines were jammed with voters keen to make sure that Oliver was cared for by their vision of one of Dickens's most loved creations. Only recently the *Daily Mail* editorial spoke about the "Dickensian" split between rich and poor in the UK, a gap that seems to be widening towards something the writer of *Great Expectations* would surely recognise.

I'm lucky enough to live in the Kentish landscape Dickens knew and adored. The school where I teach overlooks the mouth of the River Thames and the marshland where prison hulks used to lie. I can visit Satis House if I wish; I can wander round the churchyard where Pip met Magwitch, savouring the chill in the air, listening for the boom of the guns. The places he wrote about are real, as real as the legacy of his writings, as real as the images twenty million people hold in their heads of Nancy. We all know that being a "Scrooge" is not a good thing and that asking for "more" can earn you a clip round the ear. The impact of Charles Dickens seems immeasurable and timeless.

We hope that teachers and pupils will enjoy the learning activities in this study guide. They have been designed to help us better understand the impact the text has on the reader. The materials are intended for use at ages 10 to 17 (late KS2 to KS4). They can be adapted to suit the broad needs and abilities of pupils in the classroom and have been written with cross curricular topics in mind. There are also activities which explore where *Great Expectations* comes from in terms of social, historical context and literary tradition. The 2008 Programme of study, from QCA, for pupils working at key stage 4 in the UK, speaks about some vital concepts underpinning the study of English. It asks us to make "fresh connections between ideas, experiences, texts and words, drawing on a rich experience of language and literature". These resources have been created with that concept in mind.

There are curriculum opportunities for work on cultural and critical understanding, speaking and listening, drama, reading for meaning, the author's craft and composition.

This study guide can be used alongside the Classical Comics adaptation, although this definitely isn't a requirement – it has been designed to sit equally well with a traditional text.

If you would like to feedback your comments or have suggestions that will enhance this book, please email education@classicalcomics.com or visit www.classicalcomics.com for other ways to get in touch. Your thoughts and input are always appreciated.

Gavin Knight

Gavin Knight has taught English in a variety of secondary schools. He currently works as Assistant Head Teacher at Minster College on the Isle of Sheppey, Kent. Previously he has worked as Lead Secondary English Consultant for Kent, Principle Assessment Manager for English at Edexel, a Head of English for many years, and of course, a classroom teacher. He has written a variety of resources to support the teaching of English for the Secondary National Strategy, Longmans, Heinemann and NATE. He is Regional Co-ordinator for NATE in the South East, (the National Association for the Teaching of English) and is responsible for the Book Box section in *NATE Classroom* magazine.

CHARLES DICKENS 1812-1870

Charles John Huffam Dickens was born in Landport, Portsmouth, on 7th February 1812. He was the second of eight children born to John and Elizabeth Dickens, and described himself as a "very small and not-over-particularly-taken-care-of boy". Financially, the Dickens family were comfortable; and when they moved to Chatham, Kent in 1817, they sent Charles to the fee-paying William Giles' School in the area. Despite his youth, he was a frequent visitor to the theatre. He enjoyed Shakespeare, and claimed to have learned many things from watching plays.

By the time he was ten, the family had moved again; this time to London, following the career of his father, John, who was a clerk in the Naval Pay Office. John had a poor head for money, but liked to impress people. As a result, he got into debt and was sent to Marshalsea Prison in 1824. His wife and most of the children joined him there (a common occurrence in those days before the *Bankruptcy Act* of 1869 abolished Debtors' Prisons). Charles, however, was put to work at Warren's Blacking Factory, where he labelled jars of boot polish.

Later in 1824, John's mother died and left enough money to her son to pay off his debts and get him released. John Dickens retired from the Navy Pay Office later that year and worked as a reporter for *The Mirror of Parliament*, where his brother-in-law was editor. He allowed Charles to leave Warren's Blacking Factory, and go back to school. Charles' brief time at the factory continued to haunt him for the rest of his life. He later wrote:

> "For many years, when I came near to Robert Warren's, in the Strand, I crossed over to the opposite side of the way, to avoid a certain smell of the cement they put upon the blacking corks, which reminded me of what I once was. My old way home by the borough made me cry, after my oldest child could speak."

Charles left school at fifteen and worked as an office boy with a Mr. Molloy of Lincoln's Inn. Here, he decided to be a journalist. He studied shorthand at night, and went on to spend two years as a shorthand reporter at the Doctors' Commons Courts. Many thought that the institution of Doctors' Commons (a society of lawyers in London) was old-fashioned and ridiculous - including Dickens: his satirical description of his time there can be found in both *Sketches by Boz* and in *David Copperfield*.

Charles' first love was Maria Beadnell – a banker's daughter whom he met in 1830. Their relationship came to an end after three years, probably through the wishes of Maria's parents who thought that Charles was not good enough for their daughter.

Around this time, Dickens started to achieve recognition for his own written work. He wrote for a number of newspapers: *True Sun* (1830-32), *Mirror of Parliament* (1832-34), and *The Morning Chronicle* (1834-36). He was later to recognise how important these years were to him, when he wrote,

> "To the wholesome training of severe newspaper work, when I was a very young man, I constantly refer my first successes".

December 1833 saw his first published (but unpaid for) work appear in *The Old Monthly* magazine: a story entitled *A Dinner at Poplar Walk*. On seeing his first work in print, Dickens wrote,

> "On which occasion I walked down to Westminster-hall, and turned into it for half an hour, because my eyes were so dimmed with joy and pride, that they could not bear the street, and were not fit to be seen there".

He wrote further stories for *The Old Monthly*, but when the magazine could not pay for them, Dickens began to write his "series" for *The Chronicle* at the request of the editor, George Hogarth. In 1835, Charles got engaged to George Hogarth's eldest daughter, Catherine. They married on 2nd April 1836 and went on to have ten children (seven boys and three girls). Biographers have long suspected that Dickens preferred Catherine's sister, Mary, who lived with the Dickens family and died in his arms in 1837 at the age of seventeen. Dickens had asked to be buried next to her; but when her brother died in 1841, Dickens's "place" was taken. He wrote to his great friend and biographer John Forster,

> "It is a great trial for me to give up Mary's grave… the desire to be buried next to her is as strong upon me now, as it was five years ago... And I know…that it will never diminish…I cannot bear the thought of being excluded from her dust".

Not only did Dickens wear her ring for the rest of his life, he also wrote the epitaph which appears on her gravestone:

> "Young, beautiful, and good, God numbered her among his angels at the early age of seventeen".

In 1844, another of Catherine's sisters, Georgina, moved in to the Dickens household; some say that the novelist fell in love with her too.

The first series of *Sketches by Boz* was published in 1836. "Boz" was an early pen name used by Dickens. It came from

> "the nickname of a pet child, a younger brother, whom I had dubbed Moses, in honour of The Vicar of Wakefield, which, being pronounced Bozes, got shortened into Boz".

Shortly afterwards, with the success of *Pickwick Papers* in 1837, Dickens was at last a full-time novelist. He produced works at an incredible rate; and at the start of his writing career, also continued his work as a journalist and editor. He began his next book, *Oliver Twist*, in 1837 and continued it in monthly parts until April 1839. Dickens visited Canada and the United States in 1842, taking Catherine and her maid with him. During that visit he talked on the need for international copyright, because some American publishers were printing his books without his permission and without any payment; he also talked about the need to end slavery. His visit and his opinions were recorded and published as *American Notes* in October of that year, causing quite a stir.

17th December 1843 saw the publication of *A Christmas Carol*. It was the first of Dickens's enormously successful series of Christmas books which ran until 1848. It was so popular that it sold five-thousand copies by Christmas Eve – and has never been out of print since.

Pencils: Mike Collins, Inks: David Roach.

Dickens became something of an international celebrity. In 1853 he toured Italy with his friends Augustus Egg (the artist), and Wilkie Collins (the author and playwright). On his return to England, he gave the first of many public readings from his own works: at first he did these for charity, but before long he demanded payment.

From childhood, Dickens had loved the stage and enjoyed the attention and applause he received. He performed in amateur theatre throughout the 1840s and 50s, and formed his own amateur theatrical company in 1845, which occupied much of his time.

By 1856, Dickens had made enough money to purchase a fine country house: Gads Hill in Kent. He had admired this place ever since his arrival to the area as a child, and it must have felt a huge achievement to finally own it. However, Gads Hill was not destined to be a happy family home. A year later, Charles met a young actress called Ellen Lawless Ternan who went on to join his theatre company; and they began a relationship that was to last until his death.

Charles separated from his wife Catherine in 1858. The event was talked about in the newspapers, and Dickens publicly denied rumours of an affair. He was morally trapped – he was deeply in love with Ellen, but his writing career was based on promoting family values and being a good person; he felt that if he admitted his relationship with Ellen, it would put an end to his writing career.

Catherine moved to a house in London with their eldest son Charles, and Dickens remained at Gads Hill with the rest of the children and Catherine's sister, Georgina (there were rumours of Charles and Georgina having a relationship too). On her deathbed in 1879 Catherine gave her collection of Dickens's letters to her daughter Kate, instructing her to:

> "Give these to the British Museum, that the world may know he loved me once".

The more he tried to hide his personal life, the more it came out in his writing. *Great Expectations* was written around this time (1860) and includes elements of all the emotions he was going

through: imprisonment, love that can never be, people living in isolation, and the compulsion to better oneself.

He looked after Ellen until his death, renting houses for her to live in, and making regular secret journeys to see her – not easy for the local celebrity that Dickens had become. He went to incredible lengths to keep his secret safe, including renting houses under different names and setting up offices for his business in places that made it easy for him to visit her. On 4th September 1860 he wrote to William Henry Wills, the sub-editor of *Household Words*:

> "Yesterday I burnt, in the field at Gads Hill, the accumulated letters and papers of twenty years. They set up a smoke like the genie when he got out of the casket on the seashore; and as it was an exquisite day when I began, and rained very heavily when I finished, I suspect my correspondence of having overcast the face of the heavens".

In 1865, Dickens was involved in the Staplehurst Rail Crash: an incident which disturbed him greatly. He was travelling by train, along with Ellen and her mother: they were most likely returning from a secret holiday in France. The train left the track, resulting in the deaths of ten people, with a further forty being injured. It is reported that Dickens tended to some of the wounded. He wrote to his old friend Thomas Mitton about the crash:

> "My dear Mitton,
> I should have written to you yesterday or the day before, if I had been quite up to writing. I am a little shaken, not by the beating and dragging of the carriage in which I was, but by the hard work afterwards in getting out the dying and dead, which was most horrible. Two ladies were my fellow passengers; an old one, and a young one.
> I don't want to be examined at the Inquests and I don't want to write about it. It could do no good either way, and I could only seem to speak about myself, which, of course, I would rather not do".

Even when writing to a friend, Dickens still hid Ellen's name, and he didn't want to be part of the inquest in case his relationship became public knowledge.

By 1867, Dickens's health was deteriorating. His doctor advised him to rest, but he carried on with his busy schedule, including another tour of America.

Mark Twain saw him during this second American tour in January 1868 and wrote:

> "Promptly at 8pm, unannounced, and without waiting for any stamping or clapping of hands to call him out, a tall, "spry," (if I may say it,) thin-legged old gentleman, gotten up regardless of expense, especially as to shirt-front and diamonds, with a bright red flower in his button-hole, gray beard and moustache, bald head, and with side hair brushed fiercely and tempestuously forward, as if its owner were sweeping down before a gale of wind, the very Dickens came! He did not emerge upon the stage – that is rather too deliberate a word – he strode."

By the end of this tour, it is said that Dickens was so ill that he could hardly eat solid food, surviving on champagne and eggs beaten in sherry. He returned to England and despite his bad health, continued his public reading appearances. In April 1869, he collapsed during a reading at Preston, and he was again advised to rest. Dickens didn't listen, and continued to give performances in London as well as starting work on a new novel, *The Mystery of Edwin Drood*.

This novel was never finished: Dickens had a stroke and died suddenly at Gads Hill on 9th June 1870. He had asked to be buried "in an inexpensive, unostentatious, and strictly private manner", but public opinion, led by *The Times* newspaper, insisted that he should be buried in keeping with his status as a great writer. He was buried at Westminster Abbey on 14th June 1870.

His funeral was a private affair, attended by just twelve mourners. After the service his grave was left open, and thousands of people from all walks of life came to pay their respects and throw flowers onto the coffin. Today, a small stone with a simple inscription marks his grave:

"CHARLES DICKENS
BORN 7th FEBRUARY 1812
DIED 9th JUNE 1870"

THE NOVELS AND WRITINGS OF CHARLES DICKENS

These are the major published works of Dickens presented in date order.

Sketches by Boz	
Pickwick Papers	1836
Oliver Twist	1836
Nicholas Nickleby	1837
Old Curiosity Shop	1838
Barnaby Rudge	1840
American Notes	1841
Martin Chuzzlewit	1842
A Christmas Carol	1843
The Chimes	1843
The Cricket on the Hearth	1844
Dombey and Son	1845
David Copperfield	1846
Bleak House	1849
Hard Times	1852
Little Dorrit	1854
A Tale of Two Cities	1855
Great Expectations	1859
Our Mutual Friend	1861
The Mystery of Edwin Drood (unfinished)	1864
	1870

Charles Dickens also edited and wrote articles for *Household Words* – a weekly periodical, that became *All the Year Round*, for twenty years. He penned many plays and was a tireless correspondent, exchanging letters with important figures all over the globe.

He campaigned within his writings on numerous social causes –such as the dreadful conditions found in workhouses and Yorkshire's boarding schools, on poor relief, conditions in prison, prostitution, child labour, and a wide range of health and welfare issues. Because of his work he was viewed by many as being a champion of the poor; a man who wanted to reform decaying and corrupt systems for the benefit of all. At his height of popularity he was recognised as being the best-read writer in the world.

STRANGE BUT TRUE: CHARLES DICKENS

1. Dickens once scaled the slopes of an active volcano, Mount Vesuvius, by moonlight, nearly dying in consequence.

2. Dickens loved being on stage, wrote several plays, visited the theatre regularly, performed before Queen Victoria, and very nearly became a professional actor.

3. Dickens taught himself the use of shorthand aged fifteen, a skill he would later draw upon as a reporter. He completed a three-year course in less than three months. His speed and efficiency were noted by his peers.

4. Dickens kept a raven as a pet.

5. Dickens referred to his characters as his children. He said that he could see them, touch them and that he spoke to them.

6. Dickens said that he could not create a character until he had created their name: (Pumblechook, Wemmick, Jaggers, Orlick, Philip Pirrip etc.)

7. Dickens referred to himself as "The Inimitable", such was his pride in his own achievements.

8. Dickens sold four hundred copies of the first episode of *The Pickwick Papers*, his first publication. By the time the series finished it was selling forty thousand copies, such was the popularity of Mr. Pickwick and his servant Sam Weller.

9. Dickens often walked the streets of London alone at night, seeking inspiration, sometimes covering between twenty to thirty miles in one journey.

10. Dickens campaigned for the rights of "fallen women" (prostitutes). He helped set up a home for them where they could be safe and start to build a better life. He helped raise funds for many of them to be shipped to Australia for a new beginning.

11. Dickens hated child labour, having worked ten-hour days sticking labels on bottles at Warrens Blacking Warehouse in London, aged just twelve. He used many of his books to alert people to the mistreatment and neglect of children that was taking place in Britain during his lifetime.

STRANGE BUT TRUE: CHARLES DICKENS

12.   Dickens never forgave his mother, when he discovered that she had insisted that he keep on working at this Blacking Warehouse even though his father's debts had been paid off.

13.   Dickens never spoke to anybody about his time working at the Blacking Warehouse, perhaps because of the shame he felt about this time, though he wrote about it in *David Copperfield:* and in *Great Expectations* the first thing Joe Gargery did when he came to London was, "…me and Wopsle went off straight to look at the Blacking Ware'us…"

14.   Dickens toured the country with a troop of players performing amateur theatricals. He wrote, directed and acted in the plays. Money raised was donated to charities and social causes.

15.   Dickens published a notice in *The Times* stating that he would not honour any debts which were not his own – after his father started using the name of Charles Dickens as a means of obtaining credit.

16.   Dickens was in the seventh and final first class carriage during the Staplehurst rail crash of 1865. The first six slipped off a bridge and into the river. His carriage swayed about on the brink of the drop. Having helped the injured, he then remembered that he'd left the manuscript of *Our Mutual Friend* in his compartment. He clambered back into the shuddering carriage in order to rescue it.

17.   Dickens died on the fifth anniversary of the Staplehurst rail disaster, 9th June 1870.

18.   Dickens named his ninth child Dora, the name of a character in *David Copperfield*, which he was writing at the time, a character he intended to kill off!

19.   Dickens had ten children with his wife Catherine. He travelled across the globe with her and seemed happy that their marriage was held to be a model of harmony and respectability across the nation; but when, aged forty-six, an eighteen-year-old actress named Ellen Ternan caught his eye, their union was quickly dissolved!

20.   Dickens ignored medical advice by continuing to give physically draining but very profitable readings of his own works. He collapsed during his "farewell tour" and never recovered properly; he died from a stroke in 1870.

FAMOUS DICKENS QUOTES

TASK:

Here is a selection of the wise words of Charles Dickens. What do you think the quotes mean?

QUESTION:	ANSWER:
"It is a melancholy truth that even great men have their poor relations." *Bleak House*	
"You might, from your appearance, be the wife of Lucifer. Nevertheless, you shall not get the better of me. I am an Englishwoman." *A Tale of Two Cities*	
" . . . Yes. He is quite a good fellow - nobody's enemy but his own." *David Copperfield*	
"Annual income twenty pounds, annual expenditure nineteen pounds, nineteen and six, result happiness. Annual income twenty pounds, annual expenditure twenty pounds ought and six, result misery." *David Copperfield*	
"We need never be ashamed of our tears." *Great Expectations*	
"He'd make a lovely corpse." *Martin Chuzzlewit*	
"Any man may be in good spirits and good temper when he's well dressed. There ain't much credit in that." *Martin Chuzzlewit*	
"Take nothing on its looks; take everything on evidence. There's no better rule." *Great Expectations*	
". . . she better liked to see him free and happy, even than to have him near her, because she loved him better than herself." *Barnaby Rudge*	

FAMOUS DICKENS QUOTES

QUESTION:	ANSWER:
"I admire machinery as much as any man, and am as thankful to it as any man can be for what it does for us. But it will never be a substitute for the face of a man, with his soul in it, encouraging another man to be brave and true." *Wreck of the Golden Mary*	
"No one is useless in this world," retorted the Secretary, "who lightens the burden of it for any one else." *Our Mutual Friend*	
"So, throughout life, our worst weaknesses and meannesses are usually committed for the sake of the people whom we most despise." *Great Expectations*	
"My advice is, never do tomorrow what you can do today. Procrastination is the thief of time." *David Copperfield*	
". . . for it is good to be children sometimes, and never better than at Christmas, when its mighty Founder was a child himself." *A Christmas Carol*	
"The Sun himself is weak when he first rises, and gathers strength and courage as the day gets on." *The Old Curiosity Shop*	

BROUGHT UP BY HAND

Both Pip and Biddy are referred to as orphans who were brought up "by hand". Today, an orphan implies a child who is living in an orphanage, without any family to look after them; however, in Victorian times, orphans were children whose parents had both died, and they were usually looked after by family members. It was a useful starting point for a story. Not only *Great Expectations*, but also *Jane Eyre* begins with the central character being taken in by family at a young age, and not enjoying a happy home life (of course, *Oliver Twist* has the central character also an orphan, but not having any family to live with).

The term "by hand" conjures up imagery of a harsh upbringing. The opening chapters of both *Jane Eyre* and *Great Expectations* describe a very uncaring home environment, and the clever use of this phrase by Dickens suggests that the "hand" was used for striking the child – certainly, that is a widespread interpretation. However, the phrase was perfectly innocent and was in regular use.

From 1859-1861, Isabella Beeton wrote a series of articles on cooking and household management for *The Englishwoman's Domestic Magazine*. These were later published as a single volume, creating the now famous *Mrs Beeton's Book of Household Management*, in which she devoted a section to rearing children by hand.

In the absence of the nursing mother, babies could not be breast-fed. They therefore had to be nourished with milk from a spoon, or from the recent invention of a bottle and a teat (either made from rubber or taken from a calf). This hand-feeding became known as rearing a child "by hand".

TASKS:

Research Mrs Beeton online (www.mrsbeeton.com is a good starting point) and in the chapter on Children, find the section on Rearing by Hand. The language is quite old fashioned, so your task is to rewrite it in modern English, shortening it to plain instructions that are easy to follow.

For extra points, make modern-day health notes against anything that would be considered unsanitary today (hint: babies' bottles and teats need to be sterilised).

JOE'S PROFIT

Tradesmen were encouraged to take on apprentices, in order to pass on their skills and knowledge to them, thereby providing training for the young person. Apprentices were paid a small wage and in return would work long hours (around twelve hours per day), six days per week. Apprenticeships typically lasted seven years, from ages 14 to 21; because there was a cost involved, it was usual for the tradesman to receive a premium from the child's family at the start of the apprenticeship of around twenty pounds.

Pip has no family to pay a premium to Joe for his apprenticeship, but in Chapter 13, Miss Havisham says that Pip has "earned a premium" with her, and hands a bag with twenty-five guineas in for Pip to give to his (new) master.

On returning to his wife, Joe tells her that Miss Havisham has given her twenty-five pounds.

Even in Dickens's day, guineas were considered as old-fashioned. They went out of circulation in 1817, although they were still legal tender. A guinea was one pound and one shilling (where one pound was twenty shillings, making a guinea twenty-one shillings). They had a number of uses. Auctioneers would sell items in guineas and pay the seller in pounds, making a shilling for every guinea achieved on the selling price. It also allowed a guinea to be split into three equal parts of seven shillings each.

QUESTIONS:

1. Assuming that both Miss Havisham and Joe did not confuse pounds and guineas, how many shillings did Joe keep for himself?

2. A shilling was twelve old pennies. How many pennies did Joe keep?

3. There were many coins in the old monetary system, including half-penny (ha'penny), penny, sixpence (tanner), farthing, florin. Like today's coins, they were all different sizes. A famous Victorian bicycle got it's name from two coins that were in circulation. Do you know its name?

4. For extra points, think about the old monetary system compared to the one we use today. Shillings were twelve pennies, there were halves and quarters, guineas were twenty-one shillings, half-crowns were two shillings and sixpence; whereas today's coins are all based around tens. Why is this simplification important and beneficial to modern businesses?

HANDEL AND THE HARMONIOUS BLACKSMITH

Matthew Pocket doesn't want to call Pip by his proper name of Philip (or "Pip" for that matter). Instead he decides to call Pip "Handel" on the basis that:
"We are so harmonious, and you have been a blacksmith" and "there's a charming piece of music by Handel, called the Harmonious Blacksmith".

The German-born composer George Frideric Handel lived from 1685 to 1759, but spent most of his life in England. His most famous work is probably his Messiah Oratoria and, in particular, the "Hallelujah" chorus.

He wrote eight suites for the harpsichord in 1720, and the final movement of the fifth suite (in E major) is now referred to as the Harmonious Blacksmith. Handel never referred to the piece in this way, and there are a number of theories as to how it got the name:

- Handel took shelter from the rain in a forge, and was inspired by the regular beating of the hammer on the anvil, which he captured as a steady pedal note in the piece.
- Handel heard a blacksmith singing the tune and borrowed it for his music.
- There is a gravestone in Whitchurch, Edgware, for a William Powell, who on it is called the Harmonious Blacksmith. William Powell was in fact the Parish Clerk at the church (and not a blacksmith) and the suites were completed before Handel even visited the church (and long before he lived in the area).
- The most likely explanation is that a music seller in Bath, by the name of William Lintern, was previously a blacksmith's apprentice (Remember that music was only sold as sheet music as this was before audio recordings were made). He was often asked to play this piece, and he sold it as a separate item from the rest of the suite. Due to his previous occupation, Lintern was known as the Harmonious Blacksmith, and the piece got its name from him.

However, no one knows for certain why the music has the name.

TASKS:
Try to find a recording of the music, played either on harpsichord or piano.
There are many online video sites (like YouTube) that contain performances of the piece.

If you have a music group, why not learn to play an arrangement of the piece?
There is an arrangement by Chris May for four recorders on www.sibeliusmusic.com

JUMP THE BROOMSTICK

Before 1837, there was no legal requirement to record births deaths or marriages in Great Britain. It was common for the very poor to marry unofficially, in a folk marriage ceremony that involved the couple jumping over a broomstick. This ceremony had no legal status, and therefore any children who were born out of the union (such as Estella) were illegitimate.

The practice is thought to have originated amongst the Romany gypsies. A broom was placed horizontally before the door of the couples' new home, and the man and woman had to jump over it and into the home without dislodging the broom (presumably, it was placed quite low!). If the couple wanted to separate and dissolve their marriage, all they had to do was to jump backwards over the broom, out of their home, into the street. These events had to be witnessed by several people.

As an extension to this, it was considered unlucky for an unmarried girl to step over a broomstick, because it would mean she would become a mother before she married.

Interestingly, in America, the phrase is thought to have originated in Africa and to have entered America at the time of the slave trade. Of course, it could have easily entered society there through the transportation of criminals to America from England. Similar ceremonies exist in other cultures, reflecting the widespread effect of the Romany gypsies and their customs.

The broom was the only implement used to clean a house, and therefore symbolised domestic living. Women were usually responsible for cleaning, while the men went to work – which is the background to the traditional term "housewife", or put another way "married to the house"!

TASKS:

There is another term for marriage, in regular use today, which predates "jump the broomstick", Can you name it?

Today, we still talk about the groom carrying the bride "over the threshold" after they are married. Can you find out how the phrase came about, and what a threshold was? Why is a threshold so called? (hint: it is to do with early floor coverings)

CRIME AND PUNISHMENT

Like many of Dickens's books (such as *Oliver Twist*) a thread of criminality runs throughout *Great Expectations*. It isn't even treated as an exception – more like an ever-present norm – which very much reflected the way of life in London at the time. Dickens himself was, of course, no stranger to the "wrong side of the law". As a young man, his father served time as an insolvent debtor in Marshalsea Prison, and one of his first jobs was as a court reporter where he would have seen people from all walks of life. He also lived in a time of great social change, brought about by the increase in population, the impact of technological advances, the rise of industry, and the development of travel and transportation; but unfortunately, also an increase in crime.

Elizabeth Fry

Prisons underwent a change of opinion in the nineteenth century, from places of punishment to centres of correction; and the most notable prison reformer of the nineteenth century was Elizabeth Fry. A Quaker, she decided while still a teenager to devote her life to helping people in need. At first, she did this by giving clothes to the poor, visiting the sick, and running a Sunday School in her house where she taught children to read. However, she received her life's calling when she heard reports from a friend about the terrible conditions, particularly for women, in Newgate Prison (which, of course, features heavily in *Great Expectations*). Visiting the prison herself in 1813, she found around three hundred women and their children huddled together in two wards and two cells. They were forced to sleep on the floor without any nightclothes or bedding; and some of them were still awaiting their trial (and therefore may well have been innocent).

She visited the prison on a regular basis, supplying clothing and establishing a school and a chapel for them. She made sure that the women were kept occupied with sewing duties and Bible reading to help in their reformation.

In 1818, she was invited to speak to a House of Commons Committee on London Prisons. She told them how women slept thirty to a room in Newgate, where there were "old and young, hardened offenders with those who had committed only a minor offence or their first crime; the lowest of women with respectable married women and maid-servants". The committee was impressed with her work, but they disapproved of her views on capital punishment, that she said was "evil and produced evil results". The vast majority of the members of the House of Commons fully supported the existing system where criminals could be executed, even for petty offences.

However, in 1823, the new Home Secretary Sir Robert Peel (most famous for the introduction of the Metropolitan Police Force, also called "Peelers", and later "Bobbies") introduced the *Gaols Act*, in which some of Fry's recommendations were put into effect; but her work didn't stop there. The Act did not apply to local town gaols or debtors' prisons (like the one Dickens's father was sent to). Along with her brother Joseph Gurney, Fry went on to publish a book detailing the ongoing problems in 1820.

In a visit to Brighton in 1824, she was shocked with the number of beggars in the streets, that were the result of extreme poverty. Her reaction was to form the Brighton District Visiting Society – a team of volunteers who would provide help and comfort to the poor and needy. The scheme was a great success and was replicated all over Britain.

She was regularly and strongly criticised for being a woman who men went to for professional advice and knowledge. On top of that, her husband was declared bankrupt in 1828, adding to the suspicion that she was not wholly honourable. Despite that, along with the support of her brother, she continued her good work. Although prison reform was her main concern, she also campaigned to help the homeless, to improve the conditions in hospitals and mental asylums, and called for reforms to the workhouses. Elizabeth Fry's training school for nurses was a big influence on Florence Nightingale's work, and she even met with Queen Victoria on several occasions. Elizabeth Fry died in 1845.

CRIME AND PUNISHMENT

Newgate Prison

Newgate Prison features heavily in *Great Expectations*; not only because it was the main prison in London and therefore the country, but because it was regarded by many as a symbol of crime itself. There had been a prison on the site since the twelfth century (the word "Newgate" comes from the name given to one of the original Roman gates to the walled city, built around 300AD). The Great Fire of London (1667) destroyed the prison building there at the time and a new one "of great magnificence" was built in its place. This itself was destroyed by the anti-Catholic "Gordon Rioters" in 1780, when they attacked buildings that represented law and order, and in the process freed around four hundred prisoners. The prison was rebuilt straight away. The new design incorporated three areas, one for each group of prisoners: debtors, male felons and female felons. Debtors were effectively the only long-term inmates at the prison; the male and female felons were only held there awaiting trial, execution or transportation to the colonies. Prisoners awaiting transportation were mostly held in Prison Hulks that were moored on The Thames until they received a place on a ship bound for Australia.

The population was increasing, especially in the cities, and this led to extreme poverty; forcing many into a life of crime. In an effort to control the rising crime figures, the government decided to strengthen the law, making many crimes punishable by death.

As a further deterrent and as a reminder of the law to others, condemned prisoners were hanged in public. Hangings took place at Tyburn, which is near where Marble Arch stands today. "Hanging Days", or "Tyburn Fairs" were a renowned, gruesome spectacle. There were eight of them each year, and they were treated as public holidays. Crowds would gather outside Newgate Prison while a bell rang. Carts would then take the condemned to Saint Sepulchre's Church, so that they could be given their "last rites"; and from there, they would be taken to Tyburn to be hanged from the gallows. The public would follow them, and become rowdy and riotous throughout the journey, rising to a fever pitch when they finally reached the scaffold.

These "Hanging Day" processions themselves posed a threat to law and order; so in 1783 when the Newgate Prison rebuild was completed, it was decided that public hangings would take place in the street outside the prison to avoid having to move the prisoners and incite the public (the Newgate Prison gallows are mentioned in Volume II, Chapter XIII of *Great Expectations*). Hangings remained public events until 1868, when protests by many, including Dickens, put a halt to these terrible spectacles. Newgate Prison remained in operation until the turn of the century. In 1902, along with the nearby court rooms, it was finally demolished to make way for the Old Bailey. In all, 1120 men and 49 women were hanged there, mostly for burglary, forgery or murder.

CRIME AND PUNISHMENT

The Death Penalty

With the rising crime figures that were a consequence of the abject poverty, the government decided to increase the severity of the law – and particularly that of petty crimes, such as theft. Theft of property under the value of forty shillings (two predecimal pounds) carried a seven-year prison sentence; theft over that amount was punishable by hanging.

However, not everyone who received the death penalty was executed. Hangings took place in public and were attended by hundreds of people; but before long, the public started to view the condemned as heroic martyrs instead of criminals. Consequently, the number of hangings had to be reduced. After receiving the death sentence in the courts, the Court Recorder would prepare his report to the King and Privy Council.

In that report, he would indicate which prisoners should hang and which should be granted reprieve.

Murderers were hanged within two days of sentencing, but other criminals had to wait in prison for up to four months to hear their fate. While awaiting possible execution, it was even common for condemned prisoners to have the coffins that they would be buried in with them in their cells; but this practice was abolished in the late 1830s as it was considered too cruel. It was quote common for female prisoners to claim that they were pregnant (which they often were!) and force a reprieve. This was known as "pleading their belly". Instead of being hanged, prisoners who were granted reprieve were selected for transportation.

Transportation

The costs of housing criminals and the problems associated with ensuring they stayed "secured" were well recognised. The idea to ship of criminals out of Britain started life nearly two-

hundred years before Dickens was born (and while Shakespeare was still alive). In 1597, an act was passed to "banish dangerous criminals from the Kingdom", but it took until 1615 for the first

convict ships to leave England. Back then, they were sent to America. This continued for over a hundred years; but with the War of Independence in 1775, the American colonies closed their ports to British prison ships, and a new destination had to be found. The government decided upon New South Wales (Australia) and the first 778 convicts (586 male, 192 female) left Britain in 1787. The area formally became a British Colony in 1788, and from then until 1868 when transportation ended, 165,000 convicts were sent there, with only one in eight of these being female.

Surprisingly, despite the incredibly long journey of six to twelve months on crowded ships, few prisoners (less than one-in-twenty) died during the voyage. In fact, like Abel Magwitch in *Great Expectations*, many prisoners endured only a short period of confinement or labour, after which they were released "on licence". Although they could not return to Britain, many went on to prosper in their new home.

CRIME AND PUNISHMENT

Prison Hulks

When the transportation came to an abrupt halt in 1775, and before New South Wales became the new destination, a solution had to be found to house convicts awaiting deportation. The solution arrived at was to use old warships moored in the River Thames. Bought by the prison authorities after the Royal Navy had taken them out of service, these Prison Hulks went on from being a temporary solution, to become a regular holding area for convicts on their way to the New World. They were thought to be so suitable for the purpose that some went on to house more "general" prisoners; and at one point, over two-thirds of all prisoners were on the hulks. Conditions on these floating prisons were even worse than those on land.

One hulk, The Warrior, comprised three decks, each holding 150 to 200 convicts. The decks were divided into caged cells on both sides of the hull, with a walkway down the middle. Each cell housed eight to ten men, with only the old gun ports in the sides of the hull for ventilation. There were small workshops for shoemaking and tailoring onboard, which were operated by convicts who possessed those skills – however most men were used for hard labour in the docks. A large galleried chapel occupied about a third of the top and middle decks. There was a surgery, and a schoolroom. Each ward had a small library, and every prisoner was issued with a library book, a bible, a prayer book, and a hymn book. In winter, heating was provided by fireplaces in the passageways on every deck, and in the hold. The Warrior was considered to be a "model hulk" because, in response to the attempt for reform of the hulks in 1847, it was brought alongside the quay at Woolwich Dockyard and moored there permanently to allow the installation of gas lighting.

Prisoners were forced to sleep with chains around their waists and ankles to prevent them from escaping at night. Any that were found to have attempted to file away or otherwise remove them were either flogged, secured with extra irons, or put in solitary confinement.

The hulks were terribly unsanitary. Not only were there problems caused by the overcrowded living conditions, but all water was taken from the polluted Thames; and this gave rise to outbreaks of many diseases, such as cholera, "Gaol Fever" (a form of typhus spread by vermin) and dysentery. Large numbers of prisoners died from these diseases.

By 1850, the use of hulks was in decline; and in 1857, the last hulk was destroyed. Although hulks were no longer in use when Dickens started to write *Great Expectations* (1860), their presence in the book is not an error. The hulks appear at the start of the book, which is set in 1812 – a time when the use of hulks was probably at their peak.

CHAPTER-BY-CHAPTER SYNOPSIS

	Chapter 1	Pip, a young orphan boy, who lives at a remote blacksmith's forge on the marshes, encounters an escaped convict from a prison ship. He agrees to bring him food and a file so that he can remove his leg iron.
	Chapter 2	After a beating from Mrs. Joe Gargery, the sister who brought him up "by hand", Pip plucks up courage to steal the provisions. He creeps downstairs in the dead of night, to take the food and drink from her pantry, and the file from Joe's workshop.
	Chapter 3	Pip sets out for the marshes, where he is to meet his convict. On the way there he disturbs another escaped prisoner. When he tells the first convict about this man he swears that he will, "…pull him down, like a bloodhound."

Chapter 4	Christmas day festivities at the Gargery's mean a fine meal topped off with pork pie and brandy (the "wittles" Pip stole and gave to the convict). Everyone tucks in, but Pip expects his theft to be discovered at any moment – especially when the brandy is found to be watered down by tar water, and the pork pie can't be found!
Chapter 5	The meal is disturbed by soldiers who, hunting for the convicts, need a set of handcuffs repairing by the blacksmith (Joe). Pip and Joe (along with Mr. Wopsle) join the search party. The escapees are discovered fighting each other in a ditch. Pip's convict takes the blame for the theft of the food.
Chapter 6	Thinking things through, after the exciting capture of the convicts, Pip decides not to confide in Joe about the things he stole and the ways he helped the escaped criminal.
Chapter 7	Pip attends an evening school and meets a clever young girl called Biddy. Pip passes on his knowledge to Joe, and learns about Joe's early life; how this has moulded his nature and how he became acquainted with Mrs. Joe. Pip also discovers that, through Joe's Uncle Pumblechook, he has been asked to go and play at an eccentric, rich old lady's house, Miss Havisham's.
Chapter 8	He is taken to Miss Havisham's home, Satis House, by Uncle Pumblechook. He is escorted in by a pretty, but scornful girl, Estella. He meets the astonishing old woman, Miss Havisham, who is wearing a yellowing bridal dress. Miss Havisham tells him to "play". Estella and Pip play cards and Pip is ashamed of his origins.
Chapter 9	Under pressure to tell all about Miss Havisham's, Pip makes up some wild stories. He is believed by Mrs. Joe and Pumblechook, his inquisitors. Later he tells Joe that it was all lies and that he wishes he wasn't "common".
Chapter 10	Pip persuades Biddy to teach him everything she knows. Whilst fetching Joe from the pub, he meets a stranger who secretly shows him the file he gave to the convict. The man gives Pip some money and disappears.

CHAPTER-BY-CHAPTER SYNOPSIS

Chapter 11	On his next visit to Satis House, Pip meets some toadying relatives of Miss Havisham. Alone with Estella, she slaps him. Pip tells her he will never cry for her again. He meets Mr. Jaggers for the first time. He also encounters a "pale young gentleman" and fights with him. Estella lets him kiss her cheek.
Chapter 12	Pip regularly attends Miss Havisham's; pushing her about in a wheeled chair, hearing her thoughts and singing songs together. One day she instructs him to bring Joe, next visit, in order to discuss his apprenticeship.
Chapter 13	Summoned to Satis House, Joe is given twenty-five guineas to pay the costs of Pip's apprenticeship. Sad that he may no longer visit Miss Havisham or Estella, Pip reflects that he won't like his new life in the blacksmith trade.
Chapter 14	Pip's apprenticeship at the forge begins and he hates it. He imagines Estella peering in at him and seeing his grimy hands. Ashamed of his common, dirty job and coarse life, he suffers in silence.
Chapter 15	After a violent argument between Joe and the journeyman, Orlick, Pip visits Miss Havisham. He learns that Estella is now abroad. Returning home, he finds his sister, Mrs. Joe, beaten senseless by an intruder.
Chapter 16	The damage to Mrs. Joe was done by a filed-through leg iron belonging to an escaped convict. Pip feels bereft with guilt, although he doesn't think that his convict did the terrible deed. Biddy moves in to help. Pip's sister expresses a strange wish to see Orlick, and to be on good terms with him.
Chapter 17	As Pip settles into life without visits to Satis House, he becomes more aware of Biddy's intelligence and virtues. He confides in her his wish to become a gentleman. She realises that nothing will change his desire.
Chapter 18	Four years into his apprenticeship Pip learns from Jaggers, the lawyer, that he has come into "great expectations". He is to leave the forge, his friends and family, go to London, and be raised as a gentleman.
Chapter 19	Puffed up with his own importance, Pip patronises Biddy and Joe. He orders a new suit and discovers the power that money brings. He says goodbye to Miss Havisham and eagerly catches the coach to London.
Chapter 20	Arriving in the capital, Pip goes straight to the office of Mr. Jaggers. He witnesses the respect and fear people have for his new guardian. He learns that he is to lodge in Herbert Pocket's rooms at Barnard's Inn.

CHAPTER-BY-CHAPTER SYNOPSIS

Chapter 21	Expecting Barnard's Inn to be a fine hotel, Pip is disappointed to find it is a dingy quarter where he will lodge. At last his flat mate turns up; it is the "pale young gentleman" he once fought at Miss Havisham's.
Chapter 22	Pip and Herbert clear the air by exchanging all they know about Miss Havisham and Estella's personal histories. Pip learns how the old lady was deceived and jilted by a deceitful suitor on the morning of their wedding.
Chapter 23	Pip visits the home of Matthew Pocket, his tutor, where he will stay for a while, if he likes it. The house is disorganised. Mr. and Mrs. Pocket, the servants, and children seem to tumble from crisis to crisis.
Chapter 24	Pip prefers lodging with Herbert. He gets money from Jaggers to buy new furniture and sets up at Barnard's Inn. Wemmick shows him around the lawyer's office and advises him to "Get hold of portable property."

Chapter 25	Wemmick invites Pip to his house at Walworth. It is a wooden cottage, done up like a castle. He meets the clerk's deaf and much loved "Aged parent." Pip notices how his host separates his home life from his working life.
Chapter 26	Invited to dine at Jaggers' house, Pip is surprised by the attention the lawyer gives to his "blotchy, sulky" aristocratic, acquaintance Bentley Drummle. He tells Pip to stay clear of "the spider" Drummle. Pip is happy to comply. Mr. Jaggers says that his housekeeper, Molly, is as strong as any man.
Chapter 27	Joe visits Pip in London and delivers a message from Miss Havisham. He wears his best suit, calls Pip "Sir" and is ill at ease in his company. Pip hears that Estella has returned. When Joe leaves, he does not stop him.
Chapter 28	Pip decides to visit Satis House and put up at the Blue Boar. During the coach ride down Pip meets two convicts. One of them is the man who gave him the two one-pound notes long ago; he did this at the request of another convict, Pip learns.

Chapter 29	Estella is now a beautiful woman and Pip is smitten even further. She warns him that she has no feelings, no heart. He ignores this, convinced that Miss Havisham wishes them to be together. He does not visit Joe.
Chapter 30	Humiliated by the antics of Trabb's boy, whilst walking out of town, Pip returns to London. He confesses his love for Estella to Herbert. By way of reply, Herbert lets slip that he is secretly engaged to Clara Barley.

CHAPTER-BY-CHAPTER SYNOPSIS

Chapter 31	Pip and Herbert go to the theatre to see Wopsle, from Pip's village, taking part in a production of *Hamlet*. The audience holler and hoot at the players. After the show the companions invite Wopsle to eat with them.
Chapter 32	Estella writes to Pip that she is coming to London and wants him to meet her when she arrives. Whilst waiting, Pip sees Wemmick and is given a tour of Newgate Prison. Pip reflects that prison affairs seem to follow him about.
Chapter 33	Pip meets Estella off the coach and takes her to the house in Richmond where she will be staying. She teases him about the old days and tells him that they are both still the puppets of Miss Havisham.
Chapter 34	Pip and Herbert have run up debts all over London. They total them up but cannot seem to live within a budget. News arrives that Mrs. Joe, Pip's sister, has died. Pip's attendance is requested for the burial service.
Chapter 35	Mrs. Joe's funeral takes place and Pip is amongst the chief mourners. He tells Biddy that he will visit Joe more often. She does not believe him. He tells her that she has a "bad side" to her nature and thinks her unjust. Pip also learns that Orlick has been stalking Biddy.
Chapter 36	On Pip's twenty-first birthday, Jaggers announces that he is to be given £500 a year, until his anonymous benefactor is made known to him. The lawyer refuses to name this mysterious person.
Chapter 37	Pip visits Wemmick at his castle and asks how he can help Herbert make his way in the world, without him realising. Eventually Pip anonymously sponsors him into a new position as a shipping broker.
Chapter 38	Estella's life is a frantic whirl of social activities. She captivates young men across the capital but treats them all with provoking disdain. Pip is a jealous friend; he despairs when Bentley Drummle becomes her admirer.
Chapter 39	Two years have passed; Pip and Herbert now lodge in the nicer Temple district of London. On a stormy night, alone, Pip hears a noise. The convict he helped, long ago is at his door, claiming to be his mysterious benefactor. Pip realises that his hopes for Estella are all gone, and that he wrongly deserted Joe.
	Chapter 40 If the convict is captured, the punishment is death. Pip disturbs an intruder on the stairs to his rooms. He arranges new clothing, lodgings and disguise for Abel Magwitch, his guest. Herbert returns home and is sworn to secrecy.

CHAPTER-BY-CHAPTER SYNOPSIS

Chapter 41	After taking Magwitch to his lodgings, Pip and Herbert decide that they must get him out of the country, with all speed. Before that though, they want to hear him tell his life story.
Chapter 42	At breakfast he tells them all about his misdeeds, jail terms and falling in with an educated villain called Compeyson. This was the convict he fought with on the marshes. Herbert knows the name and realises it was Miss Havisham's fiancé.
Chapter 43	Pip goes to visit Estella at Richmond, but finds out she has gone to Miss Havisham without him. Pip follows her, and at the Blue Boar finds Bentley Drummle. "The Spider" gloats that he is dining with a "lady" tonight. Pip suspects he means Estella.
Chapter 44	At Satis House Pip confronts Miss Havisham and Estella. The old lady admits her deception. He urges Estella not to wed Drummle, she spurns him. He walks back to London and receives an urgent message.
Chapter 45	Warned by a note not to go home, Pip sleeps elsewhere for the night. In the morning, Wemmick warns him that he is being watched. Herbert has moved Magwitch to safer accommodation, down by the river, in the same house as Herbert's fiancée, Clara.
Chapter 46	Pip and Herbert make plans for the escape of Magwitch from the country. They make sure that they are regularly seen rowing upon the river. They feel sure that eyes are watching their every movement.
Chapter 47	Weeks pass, and in his heart Pip feels sure that Estella is now married. He decides to cheer himself up by going to the theatre to see Mr. Wopsle perform. A man sits in the shadows behind Pip. He is alarmed when he learns from Wopsle that this was Compeyson.
Chapter 48	Estella is now Mrs. Bentley Drummle. Whilst dining at Jaggers's house, Pip notices the features of his housekeeper, Molly. He feels sure that she must be Estella's mother. Wemmick, tells Pip what he knows of her story, and confirms that Molly had a daughter, which strengthens Pip's belief.

Chapter 49	Pip visits Miss Havisham and finds her wracked with guilt. She begs his forgiveness. Her dress catches fire, and she is engulfed in flames. Pip saves her but she is very badly burned; Pip's hands are, too..
Chapter 50	Whilst Herbert changes the bandages on Pip's badly burned arms, he reveals more of Magwitch's life story. He once had a child, lost to him, and whom he believes to be dead. They deduce that Estella is his missing daughter, and that Jaggers's housekeeper and Magwitch were once a couple.

CHAPTER-BY-CHAPTER SYNOPSIS

Chapter 51	Pip visits Jaggers and Wemmick. They exchange information and conclude that Pip's theories about Estella's parentage must be true. For everyone's sake, they agree to keep all of this a secret for ever.
Chapter 52	Having helped to anonymously secure Herbert's professional advancement, Pip receives a letter telling him to come that night to an isolated sluice gate on the marshes. The writer seems to know all about Magwitch.

Chapter 53	In the darkest of night, alone and fearful, Pip is set upon at the sluice gate by Orlick. He ties Pip up, says that he will kill him and put his body in the limekiln. Orlick admits to attacking Pip's sister. Herbert, Startop and Trabb's boy burst in and rescue Pip.
Chapter 54	The escape plan goes into action. They collect Magwitch and row down the Thames. A strange vessel challenges them. There is a fight, two men sink struggling into the water. Compeyson drowns and Magwitch is wounded.
Chapter 55	The captured Magwitch is bound over for trial. Herbert leaves for his new post in Egypt. Pip worries about his benefactor and his fate. He acts as best man at Wemmick's marriage to Miss Skiffins.
Chapter 56	In prison, the fatally wounded Magwitch grows weaker and weaker. Sentenced to death by a judge, his ending draws near naturally. As Pip tells him his daughter lives and that he loves her, Magwitch passes away.
Chapter 57	Struck down by illness and harried by creditors because of his debts, Pip collapses. Joe arrives, cares for him, and nurses him back to health; without telling Pip, he also pays off his debts. As soon as Pip is better, Joe leaves a farewell note, and goes home without saying goodbye.
Chapter 58	Keen to thank Joe for all he has done, Pip goes back to his village. He discovers that Joe and Biddy have just that day married. He gives them his blessing, apologises for his poor behaviour, and then leaves to work in Egypt with Herbert.
Chapter 59	Eleven years later, Pip returns to England and the marshes. He visits the forge and sees Joe, Biddy and their children, one of whom they have called Pip. He visits the site of the now derelict Satis House. Estella is there; she is now a widow. They leave hand in hand.

WHAT THE DICKENS!
A GAME OF LIFE AND DEATH

Played with a dice and counters, just like Snakes and Ladders but with a Boz Bonus; land on **BB**,
answer the question correctly and get another go!

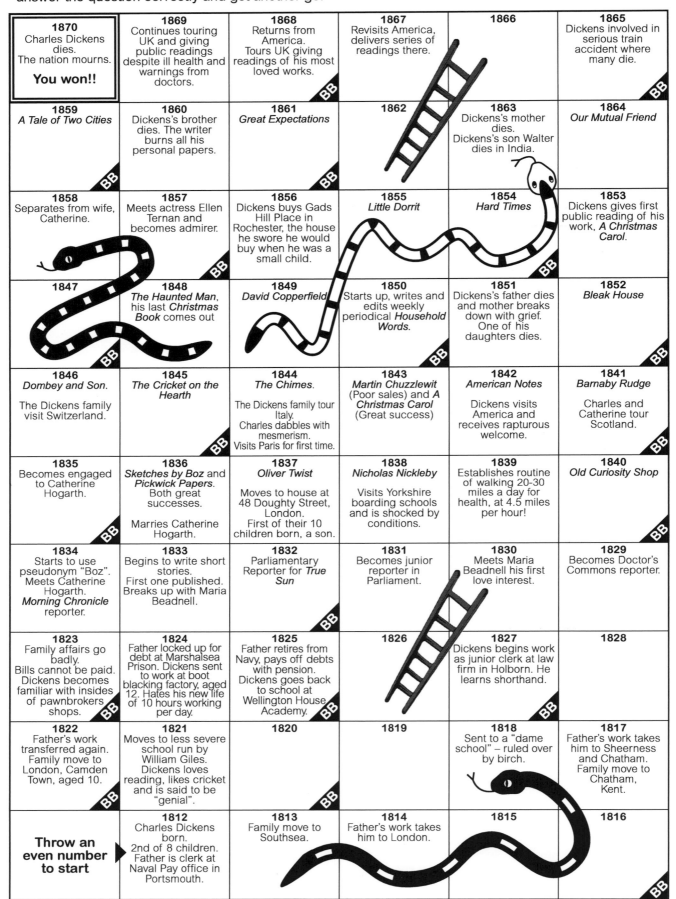

1870 Charles Dickens dies. The nation mourns. **You won!!**	**1869** Continues touring UK and giving public readings despite ill health and warnings from doctors.	**1868** Returns from America. Tours UK giving readings of his most loved works.	**1867** Revisits America, delivers series of readings there.	**1866**	**1865** Dickens involved in serious train accident where many die.
1859 *A Tale of Two Cities*	**1860** Dickens's brother dies. The writer burns all his personal papers.	**1861** *Great Expectations*	**1862**	**1863** Dickens's mother dies. Dickens's son Walter dies in India.	**1864** *Our Mutual Friend*
1858 Separates from wife, Catherine.	**1857** Meets actress Ellen Ternan and becomes admirer.	**1856** Dickens buys Gads Hill Place in Rochester, the house he swore he would buy when he was a small child.	**1855** *Little Dorrit*	**1854** *Hard Times*	**1853** Dickens gives first public reading of his work, *A Christmas Carol*.
1847	**1848** *The Haunted Man*, his last *Christmas Book* comes out	**1849** *David Copperfield*	**1850** Starts up, writes and edits weekly periodical *Household Words*.	**1851** Dickens's father dies and mother breaks down with grief. One of his daughters dies.	**1852** *Bleak House*
1846 *Dombey and Son*. The Dickens family visit Switzerland.	**1845** *The Cricket on the Hearth*	**1844** *The Chimes*. The Dickens family tour Italy. Charles dabbles with mesmerism. Visits Paris for first time.	**1843** *Martin Chuzzlewit* (Poor sales) and *A Christmas Carol* (Great success)	**1842** *American Notes* Dickens visits America and receives rapturous welcome.	**1841** *Barnaby Rudge* Charles and Catherine tour Scotland.
1835 Becomes engaged to Catherine Hogarth.	**1836** *Sketches by Boz* and *Pickwick Papers*. Both great successes. Marries Catherine Hogarth.	**1837** *Oliver Twist* Moves to house at 48 Doughty Street, London. First of their 10 children born, a son.	**1838** *Nicholas Nickleby* Visits Yorkshire boarding schools and is shocked by conditions.	**1839** Establishes routine of walking 20-30 miles a day for health, at 4.5 miles per hour!	**1840** *Old Curiosity Shop*
1834 Starts to use pseudonym "Boz". Meets Catherine Hogarth. *Morning Chronicle* reporter.	**1833** Begins to write short stories. First one published. Breaks up with Maria Beadnell.	**1832** Parliamentary Reporter for *True Sun*	**1831** Becomes junior reporter in Parliament.	**1830** Meets Maria Beadnell his first love interest.	**1829** Becomes Doctor's Commons reporter.
1823 Family affairs go badly. Bills cannot be paid. Dickens becomes familiar with insides of pawnbrokers shops.	**1824** Father locked up for debt at Marshalsea Prison. Dickens sent to work at boot blacking factory, aged 12. Hates his new life of 10 hours working per day.	**1825** Father retires from Navy, pays off debts with pension. Dickens goes back to school at Wellington House Academy.	**1826**	**1827** Dickens begins work as junior clerk at law firm in Holborn. He learns shorthand.	**1828**
1822 Father's work transferred again. Family move to London, Camden Town, aged 10.	**1821** Moves to less severe school run by William Giles. Dickens loves reading, likes cricket and is said to be "genial".	**1820**	**1819**	**1818** Sent to a "dame school" – ruled over by birch.	**1817** Father's work takes him to Sheerness and Chatham. Family move to Chatham, Kent.
Throw an even number to start	**1812** Charles Dickens born. 2nd of 8 children. Father is clerk at Naval Pay office in Portsmouth.	**1813** Family move to Southsea.	**1814** Father's work takes him to London.	**1815**	**1816**

30

WHAT THE DICKENS!
A GAME OF LIFE AND DEATH

BOZ BONUS CARD 1

Answer a BB question correctly to win another throw.

TRUE OR FALSE? **Biography:**

1. Charles Dickens was christened Charles John Estella Dickens in honour of his paternal grandmother.
2. When Dickens was a boy, he once looked out on the River Medway and saw convicts in chains being "transported" to the colonies.
3. Whilst working at the boot blacking factory Dickens met Fagin.
4. When Mary Hogarth, his 17-year-old sister in law died, Dickens kept all of her clothes and told people that he wanted to be buried in her grave.
5. Whilst touring America Dickens was disgusted by the habit of people spitting everywhere.
6. Dickens believed that ghosts, witches and vampires could be found at play during the night of All Hallows. He took to his bed and would not come out till morning.
7. Dickens once owned the stretch of railway track between Rochester and Broadstairs in Kent.
8. Dickens once acted in a play before Queen Victoria.
9. When Dickens died his last words were, "The horror, the horror!".
10. Dickens regularly drank a concoction of bull's blood and elderflower, believing it gave him extra vitality.

BOZ BONUS CARD 2

Answer a BB question correctly to win another throw.

TRUE OR FALSE? **Biography:**

11. Dickens was in France during the French Revolution and witnessed the death of Marie Antoinette.
12. Dickens had an obsession with murder and liked to visit places where it had taken place.
13. Dickens was fascinated by circus clowns and agreed to write the memoirs of a famous one.
14. Dickens enjoyed opera and wrote an English translation of *Cosi Fan Tutti*.
15. Dickens enjoyed mountaineering and climbed the Eiger whilst visiting Switzerland.
16. Dickens never drank alcohol, having seen the damage it did to his father.
17. Dickens wrote about the inside of prison in *Little Dorrit* from personal experience. He had spent a lot of time visiting his bankrupted father behind bars during his youth.
18. Dickens wrote the words to the hymn *Jerusalem* after witnessing the smoke and grime of industrial cities in the north of England.
19. Queen Victoria once invited Charles Dickens to stay at Balmoral Castle in Scotland. Whilst there he played a round of golf with HRH.
20. Charles Dickens loved watching, playing and writing about cricket. Gads Hill Place had its own cricket team made up of "gentlemen" and "working men". He corresponded with his son about the organisation of the club.

WHAT THE DICKENS!
A GAME OF LIFE AND DEATH

BOZ BONUS CARD 3

Answer a BB question correctly to win another throw.

TRUE OR FALSE? *Great Expectations:*

21. Bentley Drummle, in *Great Expectations* was modelled on Benjamin Disraeli the politician, Prime Minister and writer, whom Dickens disliked.
22. Dolge Orlick is actually the illegitimate son of Miss Havisham and her deceitful bridegroom Compeyson.
23. Herbert Pocket and Pip fought a duel with pistols, for the amusement of Estella.
24. Pip believes that Miss Havisham gave him the chance to rise in society, until he meets Abel Magwitch.
25. Dolge Orlick attacked Mrs. Joe with the same file that Pip stole from the forge.
26. When Pip wants to learn how to read, it is Biddy who teaches him.
27. Jaggers keeps the death masks of two of his former clients on display in his office.
28. Mrs. Joe believes that drinking tar water is good for Pip's insides.
29. Satis House is known by the local children as the "lair of the white witch".
30. Magwitch is "hanged by the neck until dead" because of his crimes.

BOZ BONUS CARD 4

Answer a BB question correctly to win another throw.

TRUE OR FALSE? *Great Expectations:*

31. When Pip fights "the pale young gentleman" Estella rushes in to break it up.
32. When Magwitch returns to England, he does so using the name of Provis.
33. Miss Havisham's half brother, Arthur, helps Compeyson to swindle her out of sums of money and then jilt her on the morning of their wedding.
34. Estella inherits all of Miss Havisham's money once she dies.
35. Pip's best friend Herbert is engaged to Estella when she meets Drummle.
36. Jaggers serves as lawyer for both Miss Havisham and Abel Magwitch.
37. Dolge Orlick hates Pip and tries to murder him.
38. John Wemmick is clerk to Jaggers; he befriends Pip and takes him home to meet his "Aged Parent".
39. Joe Gargery keeps a pig in a pen behind the forge called Old Growler.
40. Uncle Pumblechook likes to remind everyone that he fought at the Battle of Waterloo.
41. Joe Gargery is captain of the bat and trap team at The Three Jolly Bargemen.

WHAT THE DICKENS!
A GAME OF LIFE AND DEATH

BOZ BONUS CARD 5

Answer a BB question correctly to win another throw.

TRUE OR FALSE? **General knowledge:**

42. JK Rowling took the name Severus Snape from a brutal teacher in *Nicholas Nickleby*.
43. Dickens loved new technology and was the owner of one the first "horseless carriages" (cars) in the world.
44. Dickens wrote of *Great Expectations*, "Of all my books, I like this the best.".
45. The illustrations of Dickens's works were immensely popular; one of the best artists who worked on his stories was known as Phiz.
46. One of Dickens's favourite places in Paris was the Morgue, where he would look at the corpses with great curiosity.
47. In March 2008 the Hoosiers video for *Cops and Robbers* was shot at Dickens World.
48. Charles Dickens wrote *The Charge of the Light Brigade* to honour the soldiers who lost their lives in a fatal battle during the Crimean war.
49. The first short story Dickens had published was called *A Bad Day at Black Rock*.
50. Dickens believed in "spontaneous combustion" – that human bodies could ignite and burst into flames, sparked by heat from within.

BOZ BONUS CARD 6

Answer a BB question correctly to win another throw.

TRUE OR FALSE? **General knowledge:**

51. "What the Dickens!" Is a commonly heard phrase meant as a tribute to the great writer.
52. Dickens had a Swiss chalet built in the grounds of Gads Hill Place, where he used to do his writing.
53. In June 1865 Dickens was on a train that crashed into a river at Staplehurst. He helped pull survivors from the wreck and gave first aid to the injured.
54. When the BBC ran an audition show for the role of Nancy in a musical production of Oliver in 2008, over 6 million viewers regularly tuned in to *I'd Do Anything!* to decide upon their favourite.
55. Dickens regularly attended bare-knuckle fistfights. On one occasion he remarked that his jacket "smelt like a butcher's rag" so much blood had been spattered upon it.
56. When Portsmouth Football Club won the FA Cup in 2008, the players had an image of Dickens woven into the fabric of their shirts, for luck.
57. Scarlet geraniums were Dickens's favourite flowers. When he was laid to rest in his coffin, his body was festooned with them.
58. Whilst touring America Dickens "freed" a cotton picking slave in Georgia. George Eliot became his devoted servant and never left his side until the moment of his death.
59. Dickens was friends with Miss Burdett-Coutts, the richest woman in England and when she wanted advice about whether to marry the Duke of Wellington, it was to Charles that she turned.
60. Dickens grave at Westminster Abbey was left open for two days before being covered over with soil. In that time, thousands of people paid their respects and dropped in bundles of flowers.

WHO ARE YOU?

Can you match the characters listed below to their descriptions?
Once you're sure, put the number of that person in the box beneath the right letter.

To help you one has already been done.

1	JOE GARGERY	9	MISS HAVISHAM
2	DOLGE ORLICK	10	PHILIP PIRRIP
3	HERBERT POCKET	11	ESTELLA
4	COMPEYSON	12	PUMBLECHOOK
5	ABEL MAGWITCH	13	CHARLES DICKENS
6	BENTLEY DRUMMLE	14	CLARA BARLEY
7	WEMMICK	15	JAGGERS
8	SARAH POCKET		

A   A toady who wants an inheritance

B   A "blotchy, sulky" aristocrat who seeks wealth

C   An orphan boy with a dream

D   A gentle, caring, blacksmith

E   A deceitful suitor who jilted his bride

F   A blustering, pompous, relative of Joe Gargery's

G   A trusted lawyer's clerk

H   An author with an amazing tale to tell

I   A beautiful girl, trained up for a purpose

J   A much respected and feared lawyer

K   A jealous journeyman worker at the forge

L   A loyal friend and gentleman

M   A transported convict who makes good

N   A wealthy, bitter, recluse who was jilted

O   A dutiful daughter with an invalided father

							13							
A	B	C	D	E	F	G	H	I	J	K	L	M	N	O

WOMEN IN WHITE

Writers are often asked where they get their ideas from and whether their characters are based on people that actually exist. In 1850 an inquest was held into the death of Martha Joachim. We know that Dickens was familiar with this case.

> *"...a wealthy and eccentric lady, late of 27 York buildings, Marylebone [A large house with a walled garden] ...It was shown in evidence that ...in 1808 her father, an officer in the Life Guards, was murdered and robbed in Regents Park. A reward was offered... the murderer apprehended with the property upon him, and executed. In 1825, a suitor [for Martha] whom her mother rejected, shot himself while sitting on the sofa with her, and she was covered with his brains. From that instant she lost her reason. Since her mother's death, eighteen years ago, she has led the life of a recluse, dressed in white and never going out."*

TASK:
Try to identify five different ways that Martha Joachim is like Miss Havisham.

1	
2	
3	
4	
5	

The quotation was taken from *Household Narrative of Current Events* 1850. The same edition also had a story about a woman whose gown was set on fire and a lengthy description of the transportation of convicts to Australia.

AGE SHALL NOT WITHER THEM

The 1999 BBC television production of *Great Expectations* starred Ioan Gruffudd, as the adult Pip and Charlotte Rampling, who played a surprisingly young and attractive Miss Havisham. Somehow this felt wrong to me. My mental picture of the character was that of a wizened old lady in a faded bridal dress.

When reading fiction, we often powerfully visualise just how the characters seem to us. Sometimes watching film versions of books we have loved can be disturbing because the actors don't quite match up to the inner pictures we have formed for ourselves.

- How old do you think Pip is at the beginning of the story? (He is fourteen when he is apprenticed and he works at the forge for four years).

- How old is he when he is in London?

- How old is he when the novel closes?

Working with a partner, discuss your impressions of the ages of the characters listed in the chart below. Fill in the boxes showing how old you think they are (or would be) at these key points in the novel.

Character	Age at beginning	Age when Pip arrives in London	Age in closing sections (not the last chapter)
Pip			
Estella			
Herbert			
Compeyson			
Miss Havisham			
Biddy			
Joe			
Wemmick			

CHARACTER CHARTS

The chart below has been designed to help you keep track of your ideas about the main characters in *Great Expectations*. These blank charts should be photocopied and filled in periodically as you read through the novel.

	Character:
How the character is first seen by the reader	
Physical appearance	
Character's first feelings about Pip	
Future importance of the character	
Character's feelings about Pip in London	
Character's feelings about Pip towards the end of the tale	
What the character says or does that is memorable	
How the character is finally seen by the reader	

To give you an idea how a finished chart might look, one for Dolge Orlick has been completed already on page 38.

CHARACTER CHARTS

	Character: **Dolge Orlick**
How the character is first seen by the reader	He argues with Joe about Pip's half day holiday, claiming that he deserves one as well. He calls Mrs. Joe names when she interferes, fights with Joe and loses his job in consequence.
Physical appearance	"He was a broad shouldered loose-limbed swarthy fellow of great strength, never in a hurry and always slouching."
Character's first feelings about Pip	He hates Pip, he told him, when he was tiny, that the devil lived in a black corner of the forge. He believes that Pip will displace him.
Future importance of the character	Unclear, he is disliked by Biddy, is suspected of the brutal attack on Mrs. Joe but nothing can be proven.
Character's feelings about Pip in London	Hatred. He is jealous of the opportunity Pip gets for advancement. He loses another job, as gatekeeper to Miss Havisham, because of Pip's intervention.
Character's feelings about Pip towards the end of the tale	Hatred. He follows him to London, snoops on him, realise he's up to no good with Magwitch, sells him out and thinks he's getting revenge at last.
What the character says or does that is memorable	He arranges to meet Pip in a lonely location, attacks him and would have killed him had he not been interrupted; just as he killed Pip's sister, Mrs. Joe.
How the character is finally seen by the reader	He's arrested for breaking into Pumblechook's store, stealing his things, tying him up, attacking him and pushing flowers into his mouth. He's a villain who brings Pip considerable grief without any provocation. He seems to have no redeeming features, other than having had the strength to put Mrs. Joe out of the picture!

PIP'S ORRERY

An orrery is a mechanical device that shows the relative positions and motions of the planets and moons in the solar system. Usually they are driven by a clockwork mechanism with a globe representing the Sun at the centre, and with a planet at the end of each of the arms.

To see an electric one in action showing our own solar system visit:
http://www.schoolsobservatory.org.uk/astro/solsys/orrery/

Pip, the narrator of *Great Expectations*, is very much at the heart of everything that happens in the novel. A variety of important people come into contact with him, have an influence on his life and then move away. This is just like the movement of the stars in our solar system, with planets endlessly spinning into reach of the sun and then veering further off, because of their orbits.

The chart below is Pip's Orrery. It is not yet completed. Your task is to work out who you think the key people are in Pip's solar system at the end of the novel, and what effect they've had on him.

Label them in sequence, with the most important person being closest in orbit to Pip, and the least important being the furthest away.

Try to record all of your ideas about the impact they've had on him, in note form on the chart in some way. You could use symbols to represent the characters; an anvil for Joe, a wheelchair for Miss Havisham etc.

Put a key at the bottom of the orrery explaining all of this.

Characters you might wish to include in Pip's orrery:

- Joe
- Mrs. Joe
- Miss Havisham
- Estella
- Biddy
- Jaggers
- Wemmick
- Herbert
- Magwitch

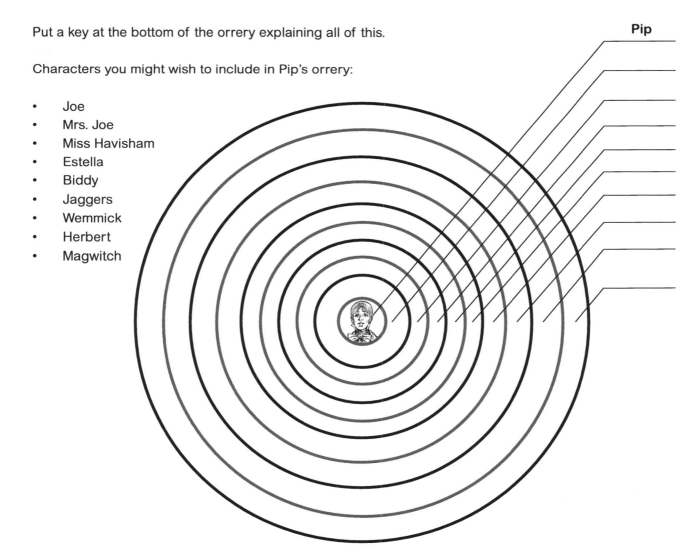

Pip

QUICK QUOTE QUIZ

Test your knowledge of *Great Expectations* by filling in the chart below and trying to identify who spoke the quotations. 60 marks are available. Some quotes are trickier to recognise than others and are therefore worth more marks. To help you, a list of possible characters is presented below. (Be warned, some characters utter more than one quotation!).

Quotation	Character name	Marks available
"Ever the best of friends; aint us, Pip?"		1
"Keep still, you little devil, or I'll cut your throat."		1
"You are not afraid of a woman who has never seen the sun since you were born?"		1
"You cannot love him Estella!"		1
"You acted noble, my boy…and I have never forgot it."		1
"If it warn't for me you'd have been to the churchyard long ago, and stayed there. Who brought you up by hand?"		1
"What have I done! What have I done!"		1
"…but as to myself, my guiding star always is 'get hold of portable property.'"		3
"On the Rampage, Pip, and off the Rampage, Pip – such is life!"		3
"I am instructed to communicate to him, that he will come into a handsome property."		3
"You're a foul shrew, Mother Gargery."		3
"He tried to murder me. I should have been a dead man if you had not come up."		3
"My dear Handel, I fear I shall soon have to leave you."		3
"Now…you little coarse monster, what do you think of me now?"		5
"I was new here once, rum to think of it now!"		5
"Four dogs…and they fought for veal cutlets out of a silver basket."		5
"And I don't dine, because I'm going to dine at the lady's."		5
"You stock and stone! You cold, cold heart!"		5
"…that there hunted dunghill dog wot you kep life in, got his head so high that he could make a gentleman."		5
"I am greatly changed. I wonder you know me."		5
	Mark out of 60:	

Possible characters:

Bentley Drummle, Estella, Pip, Miss Havisham, Magwitch, Herbert Pocket, Pumblechook, Compeyson, Wemmick, Mrs. Joe (Gargery), Joe Gargery, Orlick, Jaggers.

CHARACTERISATION:
INDEPENDENT INTERPRETATION

1. Contrast the behaviours of Estella and Biddy towards Pip in chapters 1-19.

    You may wish to consider:

    *   Who has the greatest influence upon him?
    *   How this alters his perceptions about his own situation and the people around him?
    *   Why these changes are likely to prove important to the rest of the story?
    *   How Pip's infatuation leads him to blindness about the damage he is doing to himself and the people who care for him.

2. As soon as Pip hears about his "great expectations" he becomes a different person. Examine chapters 18 and 19, show where his new found snobbery and arrogance arises, and explain whether you think these behaviours have been caught or taught?

3. At several key moments in *Great Expectations* Pip reflects on the damage his behaviour must be doing to Joe and Biddy. He knows that in his desire to become a gentleman, he has become a thoughtless, uncaring, puffed up, arrogant fool, who does things for show. In wishing to fit into higher society, he has turned himself into a hollow man, who has more in common with Bentley Drummle than he might like to consider.

    Is this a fair assessment of Pip's personality? By the end of the novel has he done anything to redeem himself in the eyes of the people he loves?

    To what extent is this novel about the need to put caring for others before caring for ourselves?

4. Joe Gargery, "a gentle Christian man", is the true hero of *Great Expectations*. He is the best model for how a "gentleman" should behave. The mistake Pip makes is that in striving to better himself, he overlooked the worth of the teaching he had already received from this "sweet tempered" Hercules at the forge.

    Do you agree?

CHARACTERISATION:
COMPOSITION

People who lived in Victorian England were often great letter writers. It was how they kept in touch with friends far away. This was not casual texting, or a swift MSN message to a mate; these were carefully constructed, stylish and detailed communications from the heart. The activities below ask you to imagine being characters from *Great Expectations* and writing letters from these people at crucial points in the story. Draft these letters carefully. If you are word processing then choose a font like Blackadder ICT, to give your letters an authentic feel.

1. Imagine that you are a young Herbert Pocket.

   Re-tell the events of the day when you called at Satis House, met Estella and Miss Havisham, failed to impress them, and then had a fight with the "prowling boy".

   Do this in a detailed, apologetic letter to your father, Matthew Pocket. If things had gone well, then you would have become engaged to Estella and heir to a small fortune. Unfortunately, they did not seem to like you, despite your best efforts, and so this scheme failed.

2. When Estella moves to London her life becomes a frantic whirl of social activity. She dines out, rides in carriages, goes to the theatre, dances at balls, and is seen in high society. All of this is part of an agreed plan. When she gets home at night she sits down and writes to her mentor, Miss Havisham, about life in the capital, and how many young men she has managed to upset during her day. She dwells on her conquest of two suitors in particular, Pip and Bentley Drummle.

   Imagine that you are Estella; write at least one of the letters that she sent.

3. When Miss Havisham's will was located by Jaggers, following her death, he also found a sealed letter for Pip, hidden within the package of papers. The letter was a record of the ways in which her actions had harmed both Pip and Estella. It ended by her begging their forgiveness for all of the damage that she had done.

   Imagine that you are Miss Havisham; write the letter that Jaggers found.

CHARACTER RELATIONSHIPS

TASK:

Draw a Venn diagram (a drawing, in which circular areas represent groups of items sharing common properties), of the character traits of Pip, Miss Havisham and Estella and the relationships between them. Put the name of each character in three overlapping circles, with descriptions of their personalities inside these.

GREAT EXPECTATIONS WORD SEARCH 1

THAT'S NOT MY NAME!

Find each of the following names and write down how many times you found each word.
If you found a word five times then write 5.

PUMBLECHOOK ( )   JAGGERS ( )   GARGERY ( )   WEMMICK ( )
HAVISHAM ( )   DRUMMLE ( )   POCKET ( )   ORLICK ( )
WOPSLE ( )   COMPEYSON ( )   PIRRIP ( )   TRABB ( )
BIDDY ( )   ESTELLA ( )   HERBERT ( )   BENTLEY ( )

```
E  S  Y  P  K  C  I  L  R  O  K  C  I  M  M  E  W  O  P  E
K  K  D  E  U  Y  D  D  I  B  E  S  T  E  L  L  A  U  R  T
E  C  D  B  S  M  E  H  P  I  R  R  I  P  O  C  K  E  T  H
S  I  I  Y  B  T  B  H  E  E  H  A  V  I  S  H  A  M  E  N
T  L  B  M  E  A  E  L  E  R  L  S  B  E  N  T  L  E  Y  B
E  R  T  C  M  L  R  L  E  R  B  T  P  O  C  K  E  T  T  C
L  O  R  O  E  E  T  T  L  C  B  E  N  T  L  E  Y  R  R  P
L  P  E  M  T  R  W  N  G  A  H  E  R  E  B  B  B  E  A  T
A  I  B  P  C  E  P  P  E  A  W  O  R  T  B  I  B  B  B  G
N  R  R  E  O  M  K  O  E  B  R  O  O  T  A  D  A  R  B  T
O  R  E  Y  M  A  C  C  Y  E  G  G  P  K  R  D  R  E  M  B
S  I  H  S  P  H  I  K  O  R  S  A  E  S  T  Y  T  H  A  S
Y  P  E  O  E  S  L  E  I  P  E  R  R  R  L  O  D  Y  H  A
E  R  L  N  Y  I  R  T  R  P  P  G  E  G  Y  E  R  D  S  L
P  Y  M  T  S  V  O  R  L  I  C  K  R  G  E  Y  D  D  I  B
M  D  M  L  O  A  R  P  O  C  K  E  T  A  G  R  E  I  V  B
O  D  U  T  N  H  E  L  M  M  U  R  D  R  G  A  Y  B  A  E
C  I  R  T  R  A  B  B  S  R  E  G  G  A  J  M  J  R  H  S
B  B  D  T  R  A  A  D  R  U  M  M  L  E  K  C  I  L  R  O
R  N  D  E  O  B  B  M  E  I  O  R  O  U  G  P  E  L  I  P
```

GREAT EXPECTATIONS WORD SEARCH 2

SOMEWHERE MORE FAMILIAR

Find each of the following places and write down how many times you found each word.
If you found a word five times then write 5.

HULKS ( )	JOLLY BARGEMEN ( )	BARNARD'S INN ( )
RICHMOND ( )	BOTANY BAY ( )	THAMES ( )
LITTLE BRITAIN ( )	BLUE BOAR ( )	TEMPLE ( )
MARSHES ( )	GRAVESEND ( )	LONDON BRIDGE ( )
DENMARK ( )	GREENWICH ( )	OLD BATTERY ( )

```
T E M P L E R Y I R B A R N A R D S I N N N G R E V E S E N D B
R T E P L E E R C S K L U H S A R J C T T I R B E L T T I L S A
D E N M A R K E O E R B D N E S E V A R G A K L H B L A E E E T
C V A Y R E T T A B D L O B M E E A B E S T N D O D T L M S B E
H U G O L B R T B L U E B O A R N E I N L I L R R I B A I A B O
C Y C O L D B A T T I R Y K H A O I R U H R L O R T H A M E S D
I A A B L U E B O A R I R A T A L M R S M B L B P T G L P M E T
W B E I U R O D P N S A D N E S E V A R G E E B R I C H M O N D
N Y B Y A R G L D B M T N E M E G R A B Y L L O J D E N M A R K
E N G B R L H O D N A T H E M U S O H D T T S N A Y R G I L S L
E A G G L E E U E N S R R H J A B R N T S T I G R R R B S D E Y
R T R R R U T D L T E O N T C E O E I K B I Y E R D H I V I H R
G O E A E A E T W K E S O A U I S L R R I L T L B E N U E H S B
T B H M O E V B A A S N E L R E W A L S M T U I J L E O L R R M
H L C N P B N E O B E R B V V D M N E R A M N T L D N N H S A B
U U I O R L U W S A D H B A A N S V E B S D E T B R I N W C M B
L E W E T R E E I E R L R B E R A I D E J M M L A N R N J I I W
K B N L L O T D L C N G O D R R G L N A R E E E R R A I O A C R
S O E D S I E U N B H D P P G E O B N N A G G B N D O S L U E H
O A E E S E H S R A M T H A M E S G T S O O R R A D B D L A N B
H R R N L G O S O D N E S E V A R G R E B E A I R N E R Y B S H
E A G M J E G D I R B N O D N O L E O M L N B T D O U A B Y E L
M B L A A A B N L L I T T L E B R I T A I N Y A S M L N A N H R
A S L R I C H M O N D A Y N N H Y N T H T L L I I H B R R A S I
H U L K S B L U E B O R E E N R U B S T N B L N N C D A G T R N
T Y R E T T A B D L O M M Y E A Y L R E N O O L N I T B E O A C
N G R A V E S E N D E E R T D A D A K N I I J E I R L M M B M O
N H C I W N E E R G G E T E B N M A Y S S Y N H C I W N E E R G
I Y T E M P L E R R T A L Y E L I N L H D M A R S E S N N N T E
S T D E N M L A A T B P N S R A D I N G R D N O M H C I R I L I
D H E N S K B B A D M A E M A R S H E S A Y B D E N M A R K I G
R A G G I Y Y B L E T V E R K A M N E D N M A R S H E S D B L M
A M A M L L D O T O A L R I C H M O N D R A H C I W N E E R G M
N E O L L L A G B R L E D N O M H C I R A A Y R E T T A B D L O
R S O O O A L T G N N H R L L I T T L E B R I T A I N R N B E L
A J J A B L U E B O A R A L I T T L E B R I T A I N H H S R A M
B N B O H M E Y D O L K A M R T O A N N K G M R D M J E M T L M
```

GREAT EXPECTATIONS – CASTIGATE ON EXPERT!

The words below are all names of important people to the story. They are presented as anagrams. Your challenge is to unscramble the letters and write the correct spelling in the box provided. To help you, the proper names are also listed below.

Jumbled spelling	Correct spelling
VISA MISHMASH	
KEPT BORE RETCH	
TENDERLEY MUMBLE	
BLOCK UP HOME	
JOY! RARE EGG	
REALLY! A CRAB	
O MY! PONCES	
OK CHEAP STAR!	
GODLIER LOCK	
HIP! LIP RIP RIP	
BE CALM HAG WIT!	
LET'S ALE!	
WE MCKIM	
EGGS JAR	
HE'S SLICK DANCER	

JOE GARGERY
DOLGE ORLICK
HERBERT POCKET
COMPEYSON
ABEL MAGWITCH
BENTLEY DRUMMLE
WEMMICK
SARAH POCKET
MISS HAVISHAM
PHILIP PIRRIP
ESTELLA
PUMBLECHOOK
CHARLES DICKENS
CLARA BARLEY
JAGGERS

DIGGING DEEPER INTO DIALOGUE

When we examine the words Dickens puts into the mouths of his characters, we can discover more about the inner thoughts of his creations. Digging beneath the surface of the language, we can expose layers of motivation and passion.

In our lives, we often say something but actually mean something completely different. Perhaps this is the case for the quotations below.

Read each quote aloud to a partner, discuss what seems to be the surface meaning, and then write onto the grid what you think might lie beneath – what the character truly means!

The first one has been done for you.

Quote	Character	True meaning
"He calls the knaves, Jacks, this boy!"	Estella	He's a low bred idiot; I'm better than him in every way. I'll make him miserable.
"She brought me up 'by hand'."	Pip	
"…I'm sorry to say, I've eat your pie."	Magwitch	
"You know best Pip, but don't you think you are happier as you are?"	Biddy	
"You and me was ever friends. And when you're well enough to go out for a ride – what larks!"	Joe	
"That boy is no common boy, and mark me, his fortun' will be no common fortun'."	Pumblechook	

GARGERISMS: MAY THE FORGE BE WITH YOU!

Much of the fun in *Great Expectations* comes from Dickens's descriptions of Joe Gargery's behaviour and the words he puts into his mouth. Joe has a unique way of speaking; he mangles and twists language, battering it until it makes some kind of sense. The quotes in the chart below give a flavour of "Gargerisms."

Can you match the Gargerisms below to their descriptions?

Once you're sure, put the number of that quotation in the box beneath the right letter. To help you one has already been done.

	Gargerism
1	"She sot down and she got up, and she made a grab at Tickler, and she Ram-paged out. That's what she did."
2	"I Bolted, myself, when I was your age – frequent – …but I've never seen your Bolting equal yet, Pip, and it's a mercy you ain't Bolted dead."
3	"We don't know what you've done, but we wouldn't have you starved to death for it, poor miserable fellow-creatur. – Would us, Pip?"
4	"…he hammered at me with a wigour only to be equalled by the wigour with which he didn't hammer at his anvil. – You're a listening and understanding Pip?"
5	"At such times as when your sister is on the Ram-page, Pip, candour compels fur to admit that she is a Buster."
6	"No, old chap. But bearing in mind that them were which I meantersay of a stunning and outdacious sort –alluding to them which bordered on weal-cutlets and dog-fighting…never do it no more."
7	"And now old chap may we do our duty...and by them which your liberal present – have – conweyed – to be – for the satisfaction of mind – of – them as never – and from myself far be it!"
8	"Which her name ain't Estavisham, Pip, unless she have been rechris'ened."
9	"On the Rampage, Pip, and off the Rampage, Pip – such is Life!"
10	"But if you think as Money can make compensation to me for the loss of the little child – what come to the forge – and ever the best of friends!"
11	"Which you have growed, and that swelled, and that gentle-folked; as to be sure you are a honour to your king and country."
12	"I'm wrong in these clothes. I'm wrong out of the forge, the kitchen, or off th' meshes."
13	"You and me was ever friends. And when you're well enough to go out for a ride – what larks!"
14	"But she wrote out a little coddleshell…leaving a cool four thousand to Mr. Matthew Pocket."
15	"We giv' him the name of Pip for your sake, dear old chap and we hoped he might grow a little bit like you, and we think he do."

GARGERISMS: MAY THE FORGE BE WITH YOU!

Description	
Telling Pip about his treatment as a child	A
Expressing thanks for the 25 guinea present which will put Pip's apprenticeship into action	B
Spotting, in Pip's slip of the tongue, the real reason why Pip is keen on Satis House	C
Showing concern over Pip's eating habits	D
Outraged that Jaggers thinks he wants money for the loss of Pip from the forge	E
Showing sympathy and forgiveness to an escaped convict who ate his food	F
Warning Pip that Mrs. Joe is on the war path	G
Praising Pip on how he looks after living in London for some time	H
Confiding why he admires Mrs. Joe despite her faults	I
Explaining why he feels ill at ease, dressed up in best suit, in Pip's lodgings in London	J
Advising Pip not to tell any more lies	K
Reflecting on the changeable nature of life with Mrs. Joe	L
Forgiving Pip and giving him something to look forward to when he recovers	M
Passing on information about Miss Havisham's will	N
Showing pride in his own child and his love for Pip	O

A	B	C	D	E	F	G	H	I	J	K	L	M	N	O
						1								

Many readers argue that Joe Gargery is their favourite character in *Great Expectations*. Give three reasons why you think people like him.

READING FOR MEANING: THE AUTHOR'S CRAFT

1. How does Dickens use language to create an atmosphere of suspense and fear within the opening chapter of *Great Expectations*?
    You may wish to comment upon:
    *   The isolation and loneliness of the young boy.
    *   The setting in the churchyard.
    *   The weather.
    *   The escaped convict.
    *   The dialogue between the convict and the boy.
    *   The landscape and colours of the marshes.

2. What impressions of London does Pip form upon his first arrival in the capital city?
    How does the writer use language to suggest that the place wasn't really, "the best of everything"?

3. Explain how Charles Dickens uses language to create the impression that Miss Havisham is a grotesque, evil old woman, eager to gain revenge upon a world that has let her down.
    Is this a fair assessment of her character?
    Does she have any redeeming features?

4. Examine how Charles Dickens uses language to suggest to the reader that Jaggers is a man of power and influence, who is not to be trifled with?

5. Joe Gargery's struggle with the English language is a comic feature throughout *Great Expectations*. Look carefully at Joe's interview with Miss Havisham in chapter 13. How does Dickens use language to make this amiable giant appear as a sympathetic figure of fun for the reader?

6. How does Dickens use language to create an atmosphere of suspense and excitement during Magwitch's flight from London?
    You may wish to comment upon:
    *   The way he describes the river and activities upon it.
    *   The night at the pub ("The Ship") and the people they meet.
    *   How Magwitch's behaviour contrasts with those around him.
    *   Events on the water once they are spotted and challenged.

ADJECTIVES - DESCRIBING CHARACTER

TASK:

From the list of adjectives pick the ones that you think best describe Pip. Once you have done this, see if you can find an example from the novel of Pip showing each quality. You may wish to add your own adjectives to the end of the list.

Adjective	Evidence
Intelligent	
Proud	
Strong-willed	
Cruel	
Loving	
Gentle	
Easy-going	
Independent	
Immature	
Considerate	
Confident	
Vain	
Kind	
Timid	
Greedy	
Heroic	
Brave	
Ambitious	
Weak	
Friendly	

CHARACTERS AND ADJECTIVES

If you are going to describe someone in detail, you need to use a large number of adjectives.

TASK:

The boxes contain the names of some of the characters from *Great Expectations*. Underneath are a wide variety of adjectives.

Which adjectives would you use to describe each character? You can use the adjectives more than once and you don't have to use them all.

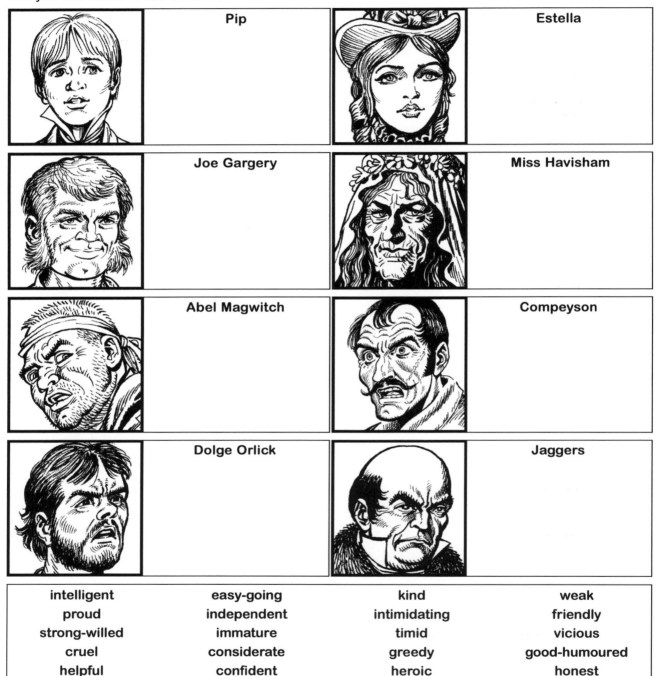

intelligent	easy-going	kind	weak
proud	independent	intimidating	friendly
strong-willed	immature	timid	vicious
cruel	considerate	greedy	good-humoured
helpful	confident	heroic	honest
dishonest	foolish	scary	naive
gentle	vain	ambitious	kind

EXTENSION TASK:

Choose any character. Find parts of the book you could use as evidence to support your choices. It doesn't necessarily have to be something the character says themselves.

WHAT HAPPENS NEXT?

TASK 1:

Look closely at the pictures on each card in the following pages. In the box, write down what you think is happening in each scene. You need to have read the novel first!

Comic Card	WHAT IS HAPPENING? Describe in your own words. Try to explain what is going on in each panel and what the characters are saying. Can you remember what happens next?
Card 1	
Card 2	
Card 3	
Card 4	

COMIC CARD 1

Great Expectations Chapter 5

COMIC CARD 2

Great Expectations Chapter 8

COMIC CARD 3

Great Expectations Chapter 39

COMIC CARD 4

Great Expectations Chapter 17

WHAT HAPPENS NEXT?

TASK 2:

Look again at Comic Card 4. Cut out the blank word balloons below and in them, write the words that you think each character is saying.

You should:
- Make sure that the "tail" of the balloon is pointing at the correct character.
- Make sure that the word balloons follow from left to right, top to bottom, so that you can follow the conversation easily.
- When you are sure that you have them in the right place, stick the word balloons to the sheet.

You could:
- Write the exact words from the novel (this might be difficult to fit in!)
- Write the words in modern English.
- Make up your own words for the characters, but make sure that they are still saying the same sort of thing to each other.
- Write in what the characters are THINKING rather than saying.

There are more word balloons than you need here. You could draw your own balloons if you prefer.

MAPPING THE LANDSCAPES

TASK 1:

Draw your own map of Pip's village, using information in the book and your own imagination as a guide. Mark on it the following locations:

- The forge
- The church
- The river (the Thames estuary)
- The marshes
- The Old Battery (a brick gun emplacement guarding the river)
- The hulks (the prison ships)
- The sluice keeper's cottage where Orlick lodges
- The Three Jolly Bargemen (the village pub)
- The gibbet-station (where criminals were hanged and left to rot)
- Ditches, dykes and embankments
- The direction of the sea (twenty miles)
- The direction of the cathedral town, four miles from the forge, where Miss Havisham and Pumblechook live
- The direction of London
- A compass
- Use a dotted red line to mark the journey made by Abel Magwitch during his attempted escape from the prison ships. Use labels to indicate where he met Pip on each occasion, where he fought the other convict, where he was captured and then returned to imprisonment.

(If you decide to use ICT to create your map, experiment with different fonts for the labelling – you are looking for an elegant, old hand-written font).

TASK 2:

Design the ground plans of Satis House. Make sure you include the following features:

- The courtyard in front
- The gate
- The brewery attached to the side of the house
- The side entrance
- The "great front entrance"
- The dressing room where Pip meets Miss Havisham
- The dining room with the wedding cake
- The brewery yard
- The small paved courtyard
- The detached dwelling house which once belonged to the manager of the brewery
- The walled rear garden
- The greenhouse
- A scullery, washroom, bathrooms, kitchen, stables, drawing room, master bedroom, library, servants quarters, guest bedrooms, ballroom, stairs, corridors, billiards room, orangery, dovecot, privies (toilets) inside and outside.

GREAT EXPECTATIONS QUIZ

Write A, B or C in the answer column.

No.	Question	Answer
1	Joe never retaliates when his wife attacks him because: a. He's scared of her b. He's so powerful, he's worried he'd kill her c. He remembers how violent his father was and refuses to act in that way	
2	Matthew Pocket was turned out of Satis House because: a. He warned Miss Havisham about her fiancé and the financial deals he wanted her to take part in b. He broke every clock in the house c. He told Estella that she had a face like the hind quarters of a cow and ought to try to smile at least once each century	
3	Biddy does not like Orlick because: a. She once saw him beat a stray dog to death with his hammer b. He dares to admire her c. He spends all his time drinking and fighting at the Jolly Bargemen	
4	At nine o'clock every night Wemmick: a. Takes his "Aged parent" out for a spin in a wheelchair b. Reads about the latest criminal cases at the Old Bailey in his evening paper c. Fires a gun from the top of his "castle"	
5	Herbert calls Pip by the nickname of Handel because: a. He's so strong he keeps pulling handles off everything in their rooms b. He painfully knows how well Pip can handle himself in a fight c. He likes some music by Handel called *The Harmonious Blacksmith* and thinks that this title fits Pip well	
6	The Avenger is the name Pip gives to: a. The bull mastiff pup he wins off Drummle in a wager b. The insolent serving boy he hires for himself c. The young man who will tear his insides out, if he does not fetch the convict a file and "wittles"	

GREAT EXPECTATIONS QUIZ

Write A, B or C in the answer column.

No.	Question	Answer
7	What nickname does Jaggers give to Bentley Drummle? a. Tickler b. The Spider c. The Red Fox	
8	Pip joins a gentleman's club and becomes a member of: a. The Finches b. The Drones c. The Masons	
9	Herbert Pocket eventually gets a job as: a. A lawyer's clerk b. An estate agent c. A shipping broker	
10	Pip and Herbert first lodge together at: a. Walworth b. Richmond c. Barnard's Inn	
11	Pip discovers that his secret benefactor was: a: Abel Magwitch b: Jaggers c: Miss Havisham	
12	Mrs. Joe was attacked (and some would say murdered) by: a: Joe Gargery b: Compeyson c: Dolge Orlick	
	Mark out of 12:	

READER, I MARRIED HER*

Victorian men were less concerned about showing emotion in public than we are today. They would hug, kiss each other on the cheek, and cry openly when moved by something. Nobody thought any less of them for this. There was a taste for slushy, sad, melodramatic events and Dickens was a man of his own time. Having planned out the final episode of *Great Expectations* he was surprised by the reaction of a trusted friend to the suggested ending. He was not happy; he demanded a rewrite. Bowing to such pressure, Dickens decided to rework the finish and offer his readers a completely different ending.

Can you work out how the original ending went?
Listed below are several possible endings that the author might have considered.
Use your skills to deduce which is the most likely original closure. (The answer is given on page 96).

TASK 1:

Recast your favourite ending from those below, either as a section from a graphic novel, like the *Classical Comics* version of *Great Expectations*, as a scripted scene from a play, or as the final pages of a novel.

1.　Estella contracted tuberculosis whilst abroad with Drummle. When Pip discovers this, he pays for her to visit the best doctors in a Sanatorium in Switzerland. She dies in his arms six weeks later.

2.　Having sought to keep Magwitch safe from the forces of the law, Pip is arrested, tried at the Old Bailey and, despite the best efforts of Jaggers, sentenced to be transported to Australia as a convict. He dies on the outward journey and his body is dumped into the sea.

3.　Drummle's marriage to Estella is a disaster. He uses her cruelly, lives a wild life, and shows no remorse for his actions. A Shropshire doctor, who has seen the outcome of Bentley's violence towards his wife, intercedes on her behalf. Drummle is thrown from his ill treated horse and dies. Estella and the doctor marry. They are poor but happy. When she finally meets Pip again she says that she is greatly changed and pleased to see him. She has now learnt what it is to suffer and understands properly how Pip must have felt.

4.　When Pip finds Estella at the ruins of Satis House, he tells her that he cannot live without her. They embrace, whilst a fiery red sunset engulfs the ruins of the building. They catch the next boat train to Calais, tour Europe together and never return to England, due to their shame at the scandal they have left behind.

* For extra points, the title of this section paraphrases a well-known quote from another famous book. Can you name the title and the author?

THE TRANSPORTATION OF CONVICTS AND THE HULKS

At the heart of *Great Expectations* lie issues that Charles Dickens felt passionately about: the law, criminal justice, prison life, and "transportation". As a child he saw gangs of convicts chained together, being rowed up the River Medway to the flotilla of prison ships, the "hulks". He must have wondered who these people were, what they had done to deserve this treatment, where they were going, and what would happen to them when they got there. His story of Abel Magwitch and Pip gives us his imaginative answers to some of these questions.

Although convicts had been transported to America since 1615, our associations of the practice belong firmly with Australia. In 1770, Captain Cook anchored his ship, Endeavour, in what is now known as Botany Bay. He had reached Australia and claimed this new land as English territory, in the name of King George III. This was a huge uncharted continent. To get the best out of this new colony, a great harbour would be required; forested terrain would have to be cut down, crops grown, farm animals bred and towns built. A large force of willing colonists would be required; people who would dedicate their lives to making this new land a thriving venture.

A lot of the work would be hard, manual labour, felling trees, digging ditches, moving rocks. This was not the kind of thing some of these colonists thought they had signed up for. The better educated, wealthier emigrants needed workers that they could order around – a group that would get these jobs done without complaint. Britain's prisons were overflowing with able-bodied men, women and children who would be just right for this sort of work. They could be shipped to these new lands and given the opportunity of a new life under Australasian stars. As convicted criminals, they could expect no say in how this new land was to be set up. Theirs would be a physically demanding, punitive life; but when their prison terms were over, they would be able to turn their hands to making this new land prosper. The first 778 convicts left Britain for Australia in 1787.

In 1786 the British Prime Minister decided to establish an official penal at Botany Bay. Shipping convicts to the far side of the world, with little hope of return, would send a terrifying message to criminals across the country. Break the laws of Britain and you could expect banishment, with little chance of reprieve. The journey was 15,000 miles across the most treacherous seas imaginable. It would take 8 months to get there and for all of that time convicts were kept in their chains.

Holed up in hulks, waiting for sufficient numbers to make the journey viable, many of the prisoners must have wondered if they would ever see their families or homes again. They must have reflected on their lives, where things went wrong, and whether there was any likelihood of escape. We know that many spent their final days before departure engraving mementoes for their friends and loved ones. Inscriptions still exist which contain lengthy poems and etchings of convicts in their boats.

THE TRANSPORTATION OF CONVICTS AND THE HULKS

Arrival in Australia must have created a new set of difficulties and challenges; the climate change, the mere fact of being back on land after such a lengthy voyage, the accommodation, the discipline regime, the harsh lifestyle and the workload.

Recent research has suggested that not all of the transported convicts were "illiterate rabble". Criminals and pickpockets, who happened to be avid readers, took books with them on the voyage, and were allowed the chance to teach fellow emigrants how to read. Some of this literate minority, having completed their sentences, rose in Australian society to positions of status. That Abel Magwitch could create such an immense fortune under these circumstances tells us a lot about the opportunities available for convicts in this new society.

Amazingly, some transported "felons" seem to have made it home again to Britain. They would have spread stories about what life was really like "down under". Perhaps the government thought that this diluted the fear of such a punishment felt by potential lawbreakers. Laws were passed making the return of a transported convict from a lifetime sentence, to an offence punishable by death. *Great Expectations* presents us with an exciting chase as Pip and Herbert desperately try to protect returned "transport" Magwitch from the noose that awaits him, should he be captured.

Charles Dickens was a man of his time. He would probably have heard discussions, debates and popular songs such as *Come All Ye Young Men of Learning* and *Botany Bay* presented on the next page, about the plight of those sentenced to transportation. These would have helped him decide that the time was right in 1861 to publish *Great Expectations*, let loose his convicts upon the marshes and see what came of it.

TASK 1:
Write several diary entries as a transported convict leaving Britain in 1800 and journeying to Botany Bay. Describe life on the boat, the people around you, how you spend your time and what happens to you when you finally reach the new colony.

TASK 2:
Working in a group of four to six, produce a choral reading of the songs *Come All Ye Young Men of Learning* and *Botany Bay*. You might decide to turn them into rap songs and beat out the rhythm on your desks. (If you want to hear how the melodies traditionally sound visit: http://ingeb.org/songs/botanyba.html).

THE TRANSPORTATION OF CONVICTS AND THE HULKS

Come All Ye Young Men of Learning

Come all ye young men of learning,
And a warning take from me,
I would have you quit night walking,
And shun bad company,
I would have you quit night walking,
Or else you'll rue the day,
You'll rue your transportation, lads,
When you're bound for Botany Bay.

I was brought up in London town,
At a place I know full well,
Brought up by honest parents,
For the truth to tell.
Brought up by honest parents,
And reared most tenderly,
Till I became a roving blade,
Which proved my destiny.

My character was shaken,
And I was sent to jail.
My friends they tried to clear me,
But nothing could prevail.
At the old Bailey sessions,
The judge to me did say:
The jury found you guilty, lad,
So you go to Botany Bay.

It was on May the twenty eight,
From England we did steer,
And all things being safe on board,
We sailed down the river clear.
And every ship that we passed by,
We heard the sailors say:
Good thing it's them not us, ho! ho!
That are bound for Botany Bay.

To see my poor old father,
As he stood at the bar.
Likewise my dear old mother,
Her old gray locks she tore,
And in tearing of her old gray locks.
These words to me she did say,
O son ! O son ! What hast thou done,
Thou art bound for Botany Bay.

There is a girl in Manchester,
A girl I know quite well,
And if I ever get set free,
With her I intend to dwell.
Which means, I mean to marry her,
And no more go astray,
I'll shun all evil company,
Bid adieu to Botany Bay.

Botany Bay

Farewell to old England forever.
Farewell to my rum culls as well.
Farewell to the well known Old Bailey.
Where I used for to cut such a swell.

Singing Tooral liooral liaddity.
Singing Tooral liooral liay.
Singing Tooral liooral liaddity.
And we're bound for Botany Bay.

There's the captain as is our commander.
There's the bosun and all the ship's crew.
There's the first and the second class passengers.
Knows what we poor convicts go through.

Taint leaving old England we cares about.
Taint cos we mis-spells what we knows.
But because all we light fingered gentry.
Hops around with a log on our toes.

These seven long years I've been serving now.
And seven long more have to stay.
All for bashing a bloke down our alley.
And taking his ticker away.

Oh had I the wings of a turtle dove.
I'd soar on my pinions so high.
Slap bang to the arms of my Polly love.
And in her sweet presence I'd die.

Now all my young Dookies and Dutchesses.
Take warning from what I've to say.
Mind all is your own as you toucheses.
Or you'll find us in Botany Bay.

CHARACTER AND MOTIVATION

TASK 1:

Below is an example of a mind map. Present all the characters in the novel and their relationships in the form of a mind map. Use one of the images from the book in the centre of the page to start you off. Pick a central character. Now draw lines to the other characters showing who is related to whom, how they are connected in other ways and any other "joining" threads you can think of. Explain the connections, using quotes where you can.

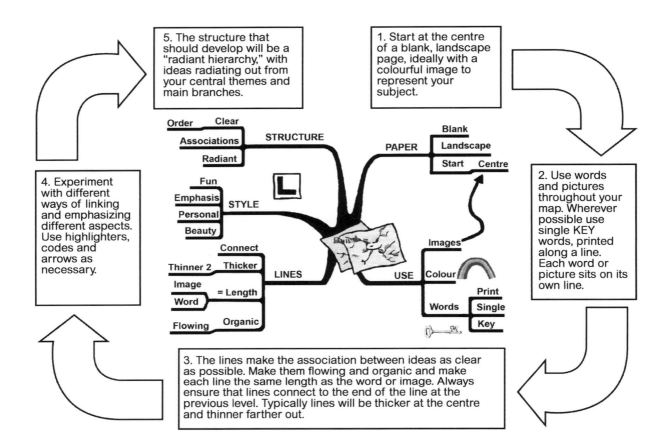

TASK 2:

Imagine the characters are pieces on a chessboard. Working in pairs, decide which characters would be the king, the queen, the knight and so forth. Compare your findings with other pairs.

TASK 3:

Working in pairs or groups, design a set of Top Trumps cards for the characters in the book. Decide what you will base the points ratings on.

'TWAS THE NIGHT BEFORE CHRISTMAS

SCENARIO:

Imagine that it is Christmas Eve. Miss Havisham is having trouble sleeping. Estella has been abroad at her "finishing" school for four years. Pip is apprenticed at the forge and never comes to visit. She is lonely and upset.

In the hour before midnight, she is visited in turn by three spirits; the ghosts of Christmas past, Christmas present, and Christmas future. They show her how her life has gone wrong and what will happen if she doesn't change her ways.

As the clock, which has been stopped at twenty minutes to nine for many years, mysteriously starts up and chimes midnight, she decides to change her ways.

Satis House will become a place of joy and light, everything will alter.

TASK:

Script, or improvise, what happens that night and the following morning. Rehearse and then perform your play to the rest of your class.

THE GOOD SHEPHERD

SCENARIO:

Fifteen thousand miles away from his birthplace, Magwitch became a shepherd. He used to work on his own, far away from the company of men and women. To stop himself from going mad, he used to talk to his sheep. He told them all about his early life, his misdeeds, his hatred for Compeyson, his time under lock and key in the "hulks", his escape and the "dear boy" who helped him. He told his flock all about his dream to turn that lowly lad on the marshes into a fine gentleman.

TASK:

Script, or improvise, what happens one night when he lights up his pipe and tells his woolly audience all about his life. Rehearse and then perform your play to the rest of your class. Use class members to act out his history while the central character narrates his tale.

ALL YOU NEED IS LOVE

SCENARIO:

When Pip hears from Joe that Estella has returned to England, he decides to visit Satis House with all speed. He catches the next coach down to Kent and puts up at The Blue Boar. He stays there rather than at the forge to avoid being an "inconvenience" to everyone at Joe's dwelling.

He believes Miss Havisham to be his mysterious benefactor. He thinks she has turned him into a gentleman so that he can marry Estella, enabling him to:

> "…restore the desolate house, admit sunshine into the dark rooms, tear down the cobwebs, destroy the vermin… do…shining deeds…and marry the princess."

With his head full of these romantic thoughts and great expectations, imagine that Pip bumps into Biddy in the town. Unaware that he has caused any offence, he takes her to a coffee shop and pours out his heart and soul to her. He reveals all of his hopes and dreams.

Biddy is far wiser about people and their motives than Pip. She realises that he is heading for a fall. She tries to warn him, but he will not listen. He thinks that she's jealous of his good fortune and jealous of his love for Estella. He warns her not to interfere and to tell nobody about their private conversation. He storms out of the coffee shop wishing that he'd never confided in her.

TASK:

Script, or improvise, what happens when they meet and have this discussion. Rehearse and then perform your play to the rest of your class.

THE FROG PRINCE FROM THE MARSH

SCENARIO:

A newspaper reporter from *The Evening Chronicle* hears something about Pip's remarkable rise from rags to riches at a party in London. Curious, he decides to do some investigating; he senses that there might be a good story in this. Unsure what angle he wants to take in his reporting, he tracks down some "friends" of Pip.

They are:
- Mr. Pumblechook
- Sarah Pocket
- Trabb's boy
- Orlick
- The Avenger
- Bentley Drummle

TASK 1:

In groups of four to six, identify pupils to be questioned in the role of each of the above characters. Hot seat/interview each person in turn, making sure you find out:

- what they know about Pip's rise to riches
- when and where they first came into contact with Pip
- how they felt about him then
- what they feel about him now
- why everybody appears to dislike him

SCENARIO:

Everybody the journalist interviewed seemed to loathe Pip. They gave him lots of dirt about Pip's history, behaviour and life style in London. In the end the reporter printed his story in the gossip column. It ran under the heading *The Frog Prince from the Marsh*. When Pip read it he was deeply upset. He could not believe some of the things that people had said about him. He showed it to Herbert, when he returned to their rooms at Barnard's Inn that night. Pip's best friend had a difficult job on his hands to calm him down and make him see sense about the views expressed.

TASK 2:

Script, or improvise, what happened when Pip and Herbert discussed this newspaper article. Rehearse and then perform your play to the rest of your class.

ALAS POOR ORLICK!

SCENARIO:

At the end of the novel, Orlick has been arrested and put into the County Jail for breaking into Pumblechook's house: drinking his wine, stealing his food, slapping his face, tying him up and putting flowers into his mouth.

After further investigation, he is also charged with the murder of Mrs. Joe Gargery, and the attempted murder of Mr. Philip Pirrip (Pip).

Jaggers is hired to be the Chief Prosecutor. The trial is to take place at the Old Bailey. If found guilty, the defendant, Dolge Orlick, will be hanged by the neck until dead.

On the night before the trial commences, Pip receives a note from Wemmick asking him to go to Newgate Prison. When he gets there he discovers that Orlick wishes to speak with him. Uneasy about what might happen, he asks Wemmick to come into the prison cell with him.

TASK 1:

Script, or improvise, what happens when they go into the prison cell.
Rehearse and then perform your play to the rest of your class.

TASK 2:

Script or improvise, what happens when Orlick takes the stand, during his trial, and is cross-examined by Jaggers. Rehearse and then perform your play to the rest of your class.

TASK 3:

Script or improvise, what happens when Pip takes the stand, during the trial, and is cross-examined by Jaggers. Rehearse and then perform your play to the rest of your class.

TASK 4:

As a class, having heard the evidence, act as jurors and decide whether Dolge Orlick is guilty or not guilty of these crimes. Select someone to act as the Judge and pass an appropriate sentence on the defendant.

GUIDED TOURS

SCENARIO:

(Your teacher might wish to identify and play suitable background music whilst the tours take place)

Satis House

In pairs, Person **A** (with eyes open) leads Person **B** (with eyes closed) into Satis House through the side door Pip uses when he visits.

Person **A**: provide a spoken commentary as you move along the corridors, up the stairs and through the various empty and abandoned rooms in the house.
The tour ends in the room containing the dining table and the rotting wedding cake.

The roles are then reversed, and the tour continues downstairs once more, out into the garden and then across the courtyard towards the Brewery.

Person **B**: (with eyes open) describe the view to Person **A** (with eyes closed) as you move through the overgrown garden, find the old greenhouse, and then look into the fenced off courtyard with the rotten barrels. The tour ends when you see a strange object dangling from a beam in the old brewery that looks suspiciously like an old lady, hanging from a rope!

(Read chapter 8 again if you need a reminder of how things look).

The Forge

In pairs, Person **A** (with eyes open) leads Person **B** (with eyes closed) into the house where Pip lives as a child.

Person **A**: provide a spoken commentary as you move in through the front door and into the scullery, kitchen, dining room and various bedrooms in the house. The tour halts in Pip's bedroom, when you find a strange book under his bed.

The roles are then reversed and the tour continues downstairs once more, into the cellar, and then out and around the garden before going into the forge.

Person **B**: (with eyes open) describe the view to Person **A** (with eyes closed) as you move through the cottage garden, past the hens and livestock, (watch out for the pig poo!), and then look into the forge and see the glowing coals. Step inside and feel the heat. Explain what you can about the various blacksmith's tools hanging up and leaning against the walls. The tour ends when you see and describe the blacksmith, who is at the end of the lane checking the shoes of a mighty carthorse.

FREEZE FRAME SEQUENCING

In groups of four to six people, identify five key moments from the final chapters of *Great Expectations* which you think are very important.

You might choose some of the following:

- Pip saving Miss Havisham from the flames
- Magwitch's attempt to escape from London on the river
- The capture of Magwitch
- The sentencing of Magwitch
- The final moments of Magwitch's life
- Pip's illness striking him down
- Joe's nursing of Pip
- The marriage of Joe and Biddy
- Pip and Estella, together again, in the grounds of Satis House

Remind yourselves how Dickens described these moments.

In your groups, you are going to recreate these scenes as a sequence of freeze frame images.

- For each image you will need to decide how the characters might be standing, or sitting, where their arms will be, and what their facial expressions will be.

Remember that you are going to put on these freeze frame images for the rest of your class.
Discuss each moment carefully, and practice until you're sure it's right.
When ready, count down from five and hold each pose rigidly. **Don't move! Don't speak!**

Peer assessment:

Comment on the strengths of the other groups' freeze frame sequences, together with one area for possible development and improvement.

Extension opportunities: ICT presentation(s)

Using a digital camera, get somebody to photograph each pose in your freeze frame sequence. Upload the images to a PC or laptop, paste your photos into a slideshow presentation, and then show this to your teacher and the rest of the class. For each shot, you will need to be able to explain your thoughts on how your frozen image relates to the key moment in *Great Expectations*.

Alternatively, if you have the resources and ICT skills, you could import all of your freeze frame images into Windows Moviemaker or Microsoft Photo Story and use them as slides to create a brief trailer for an exciting new film version of *Great Expectations*!

COLOUR ME IN

COLOUR ME IN

COLOUR ME IN

COLOUR ME IN

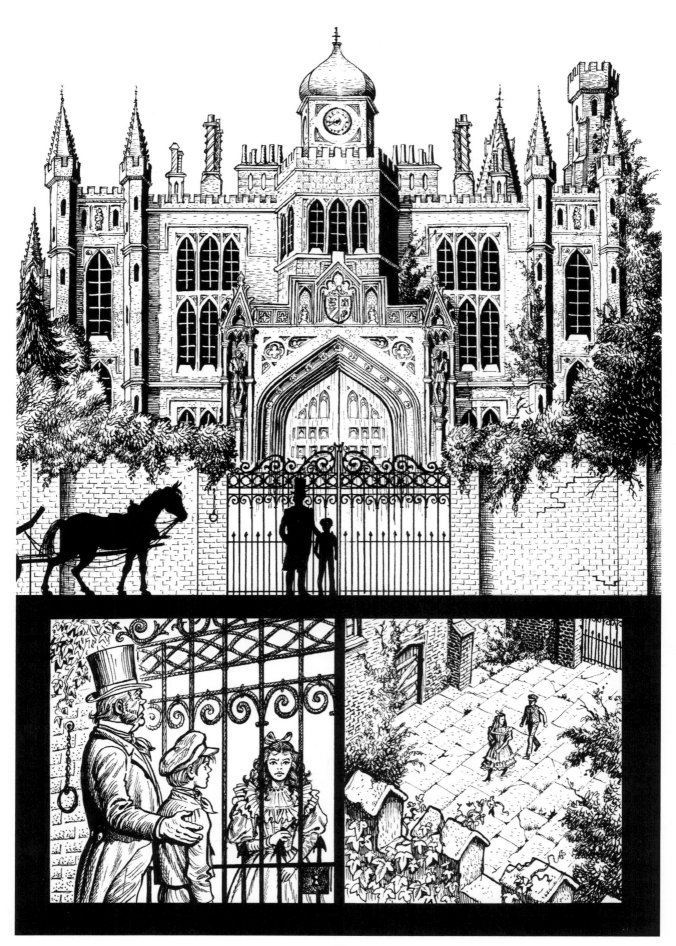

FILM VERSIONS

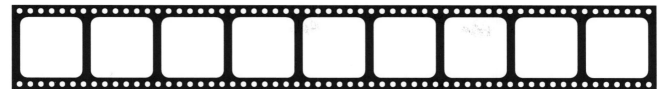

In 1946 David Lean directed a stunning adaptation of *Great Expectations*. Lasting one hundred and eighteen minutes, it won two Oscars and was nominated for another three. John Mills played the adult Pip, Alec Guiness was Herbert Pocket and Jean Simmons shone as the young Estella. Shot entirely in black and white, this atmospheric masterpiece **must be seen** by any pupil working on the novel!

Warnings:

1. Seeing films is not the same as reading books. David Lean leaves out lots of key events, drops some important characters and often changes perspective to create his own interpretation. Speaking about the process of creating an adaptation from literature he said,

    "Choose what you want to do in the novel and do it proud. If necessary cut characters. Don't keep every character, just take a sniff of each one."

2. Your teacher will have seen this film. If you're working on an assignment in class, a coursework piece, or an assessment of some kind – don't write about the talking cows, or anything else memorable from David Lean's film. Stick to the book Charles Dickens wrote when writing your comments!

3. Once you've seen Finlay Currie as Magwitch, you won't be able to picture any other escaping convict inside your head!

4. Two dreadful puns on names are included on this page. Can you spot them?
    (See Page 96 for the solution.)

Kevin Connor directed a television mini-series based on the book for Disney Channel in 1989. Praised for its authenticity to Dickens's text, it starred Jean Simmons, John Rhys Davies and Ray McAnally.

In 1998 Alfonso Cuarón directed a remarkable version of *Great Expectations*, which was updated to the 1970s and set in Florida and New York. Gwyneth Paltrow and Ethan Hawke play Estella and Pip (renamed Finn in this version), whilst Robert De Niro is an escaped convict. The film lasts one hundred and eleven minutes and had a certificate "15" because of some swearing and a steamy sex scene. This interpretation is certainly worth seeing, for viewers aged fifteen or above, and should lead to some interesting thoughts and discussion on how film directors rework the characters, themes and landscapes of Charles Dickens.

A silent film version was released in America in 1917, directed by Robert G. Vignola and Paul West. Surprisingly, this is still available via the Internet Movie Database. In 1934 Universal Studios brought out a "talking picture" of the book directed by Stuart Walker. This too is available to buy but reviewers consider it to be vastly inferior to David Lean's remake.

Channel 4 Education made a helpful programme looking at different film versions and comparing them to the original text. Entitled *The English Programme: Not as Good as the Book: Great Expectations* it is still regularly scheduled for broadcasting. To find out more visit the Channel 4 website at:
http://www.channel4learning.com/index.html

BOOK REPORT

A book report summarises the content of a book. Write a book report about *Great Expectations*.

Name: _____

Date: _____

Book Title: _____
Author: _____
Artwork: _____
Publisher: _____
Copyright: _____
No of Pages: _____

Characters: Who were the main characters?
_____
_____
_____
_____
_____
_____
_____
_____

Setting: Where and when was the book set?
_____
_____
_____
_____
_____
_____
_____
_____

Plot: What happens in the book?
_____
_____
_____
_____
_____
_____
_____
_____
_____

Did you like or dislike the book? Explain why.
_____
_____
_____
_____
_____
_____
_____
_____
_____
_____
_____
_____

What new words or facts did you learn?
_____
_____
_____
_____
_____
_____
_____
_____
_____
_____

Ending: What happens at the end?
_____
_____
_____
_____
_____

BOOK REVIEW

A book review is more detailed than a book report and assesses the book's strengths and weaknesses. When writing your review of *Great Expectations* think about these:

- Did you find the book interesting?
- Did the format of the book help you to understand what was happening?
- What was your reaction to the story?
- Did you learn anything?
- What would you have done differently to Charles Dickens?
- Would you recommend this book to others?

Continue on a separate sheet if you need to.

Book Title: _____
Author: _____
Artwork: _____
Publisher: _____
Copyright: _____
No of Pages: _____

Once your review is finished you could upload it to one of the many book review websites such as:

www.amazon.co.uk   www.whosreadit.com
www.kidsreview.org.uk   www.mrsmad.com
www.cool-reads.co.uk

Book Review:
_____
_____
_____
_____
_____
_____
_____
_____
_____
_____
_____
_____
_____
_____
_____
_____
_____
_____
_____
_____
_____
_____
_____
_____
_____

Name: _____
Date: _____

FAMOUS DICKENS QUOTES
TEACHERS' VERSION

Solution: (Page: 14)

QUESTION:	ANSWER:
"It is a melancholy truth that even great men have their poor relations." *Bleak House*	It doesn't matter how rich or important you are…everyone has someone in their family who might very well embarrass them!
"You might, from your appearance, be the wife of Lucifer. Nevertheless, you shall not get the better of me. I am an Englishwoman." *A Tale of Two Cities*	This could be taken two ways (at least). One interpretation is that Dickens makes fun of the stereotypical resilience ("stiff upper lip") of the English. A second is that he genuinely admires the strength of the English character, especially in the female form.
" . . . Yes. He is quite a good fellow - nobody's enemy but his own." *David Copperfield*	A play upon "you are your own worst enemy". The individual causes more problems for themselves than anyone else might do.
"Annual income twenty pounds, annual expenditure nineteen pounds nineteen and six, result happiness. Annual income twenty pounds, annual expenditure twenty pounds ought and six, result misery." *David Copperfield*	Dickens considers the narrow margins on which happiness can change into misery for many people. Paying the bills keeps people off your back and you are still your own master (or mistress!). Financial independence is one major key to happiness.
"We need never be ashamed of our tears." *Great Expectations*	Many people, especially men, are ashamed of expressing emotion and Dickens argues here that this is a mistake. In fact, not to cry at times might be a source of shame.
"He'd make a lovely corpse." *Martin Chuzzlewit*	A fantastic quote as it is in the form of a compliment but betrays the deepest hatred for someone. The speaker imagines the subject of their quote as being dead and takes great pleasure in the idea.
"Any man may be in good spirits and good temper when he's well dressed. There ain't much credit in that." *Martin Chuzzlewit*	A common theme for Dickens and one which was later taken up by the likes of Kipling. A man's true character is not revealed when things are going well, but when he is suffering adversity. The adversity expressed here, typically, would be poverty.
"Take nothing on its looks; take everything on evidence. There's no better rule." *Great Expectations*	Wise words indeed! It is easy to be deceived by appearances in all manner of circumstances. Beliefs should be formed on the basis of actions and attributes rather than appearances!
" . . . she better liked to see him free and happy, even than to have him near her, because she loved him better than herself." *Barnaby Rudge*	An indicator of true love is when someone puts another's interests and happiness above their own. In this quote, the woman is prepared to let her love interest seek his happiness elsewhere, because knowing he would be happier that way exceeds the happiness she would feel for herself in having him near.

FAMOUS DICKENS QUOTES
TEACHERS' VERSION

Solution: (Page: 15)

QUESTION:	ANSWER:
"I admire machinery as much is any man, and am as thankful to it as any man can be for what it does for us. But it will never be a substitute for the face of a man, with his soul in it, encouraging another man to be brave and true." *Wreck of the Golden Mary*	Dickens, long before Orwell, is indicating the advance of the "machine". Although he sees the benefits, he is well aware that, for all the improvements technology might bring, there will always be a need for the involvement of people.
"No one is useless in this world," retorted the Secretary, "who lightens the burden of it for any one else." *Our Mutual Friend*	There is a general Christian theme running through much of Dickens's writing, and the value of helping others is reflected here. Although one might feel worthless, there is great worth in the act of helping others.
"So, throughout life, our worst weaknesses and meannesses are usually committed for the sake of the people whom we most despise." *Great Expectations*	Again, like all good quotes, this encompasses a general truth. Negative emotions and actions, which reflect badly on the individual, are often a direct result of people we don't like.
"My advice is, never do tomorrow what you can do today. Procrastination is the thief of time." *David Copperfield*	Another simple piece of advice. The sentiment isn't original to Dickens, but this form of words is. In other words, get on with it! Time wasting is a crime!
". . . for it is good to be children sometimes, and never better than at Christmas, when its mighty Founder was a child himself." *A Christmas Carol*	When people grow older it is inevitable that they lose some of the genuine wonder and excitement which children naturally possess. There are many benefits in returning to a child's mindset now and again. Dickens also makes another link to Christianity.
"The Sun himself is weak when he first rises, and gathers strength and courage as the day gets on." *The Old Curiosity Shop*	The metaphor of the sun is particularly apt as it starts weak, and goes on to be strong. It is yet another piece of advice for those people who might be suffering.

BROUGHT UP BY HAND
TEACHERS' VERSION

(From Page: 16) Here is the extract from Mrs Beeton's book:

Articles necessary, and how to use them,—Preparation of Foods.— Baths.—Advantages of Rearing by Hand.

2497.   As we do not for a moment wish to be thought an advocate for an artificial, in preference to the natural course of rearing children, we beg our renders to understand us perfectly on this head; all we desire to prove is the fact that a child can be brought up as well on a spoon dietary as the best example to be found of those reared on the breast; having more strength, indeed, from the more nutritious food on which it lives. It will be thus less liable to infectious diseases, and more capable of resisting the virulence of any danger that may attack it; and without in any way depreciating the nutriment of its natural food, we wish to impress on the mother's mind that there are many cases of infantine debility which might eventuate in rickets, curvature of the spine, or mesenteric disease, where the addition to, or total substitution of, an artificial and more stimulating aliment, would not only give tone and strength to the constitution, but at the same time render the employment of mechanical means totally unnecessary. And, finally, though we would never—where the mother had the strength to suckle her child—supersede the breast, we would insist on making it a rule to accustom the child as early as possible to the use of an artificial diet, not only that it may acquire more vigour to help it over the ills of childhood, but that, in the absence of the mother, it might not miss the maternal sustenance; and also for the parent's sake, that, should the milk, from any cause, become vitiated, or suddenly cease, the child can be made over to the bottle and the spoon without the slightest apprehension of hurtful consequences.

2498.   To those persons unacquainted with the system, or who may have been erroneously informed on the matter, the rearing of a child by hand may seem surrounded by innumerable difficulties, and a large amount of personal trouble and anxiety to the nurse or mother who undertakes the duty. This, however, is a fallacy in every respect, except as regards the fact of preparing the food; but even this extra amount of work, by adopting the course we shall lay down, may be reduced to a very small sum of inconvenience; and as respects anxiety, the only thing calling for care is the display of judgment in the preparation of the food. The articles required for the purpose of feeding an infant are a night-lamp, with its pan and lid, to keep the food warm; a nursing-bottle, with a prepared teat; and a small pap saucepan, for use by day. Of the lamp we need hardly speak, most mothers being acquainted with its operation: but to those to whom it is unknown we may observe, that the flame from the floating rushlight heats the water in the reservoir above, in which the covered pan that contains the food floats, keeping it at such a heat that, when thinned by milk, it will be of a temperature suitable for immediate use. Though many kinds of nursing-bottles have been lately invented, and some mounted with India-rubber nipples, the common glass bottle, with the calf's teat, is equal in cleanliness and utility to any; besides, the nipple put into the child's mouth is so white and natural in appearance, that no child taken from the breast will refuse it. The black artificial ones of caoutchouc or gutta-percha are unnatural. The prepared teats can be obtained at any chemist's, and as they are kept in spirits, they will require a little soaking in warm water, and gentle washing, before being tied securely, by means of fine twine, round the neck of the bottle, just sufficient being left projecting for the child to grasp freely in its lips; for if left the full length, or over long, it will be drawn too far into the mouth, and possibly make the infant heave. When once properly adjusted, the nipple need never be removed till replaced by a new one, which will hardly be necessary oftener than once a fortnight, though with care one will last for several weeks. The nursing-bottle should be thoroughly washed and cleaned every day, and always rinsed out before and after using it, the warm water being squeezed through the nipple, to wash out any particles of food that might lodge in the aperture, and become sour. The teat can always be kept white and soft by turning the end of the bottle, when not in use, into a narrow jug containing water, taking care to dry it first, and then to warm it by drawing the food through before putting it into the child's mouth.

JOE'S PROFIT
TEACHERS' VERSION

Solution: (Page: 17)

1.   Joe kept twenty-five shillings
2.   25 x 12 = 300 pennies
3.   The penny-farthing.
4.   Not only is it simpler to understand, it would be incredibly difficult to build computer systems to cope with such a varied system. Data entry of these peculiar values would be complex – imagine Internet shopping using a base-twelve system! Crossing over between other currencies would be difficult, too. In hindsight, the 1971 decimalisation of UK currency facilitated modern multi-national businesses.

JUMP THE BROOMSTICK
TEACHERS' VERSION

Solution: (Page: 19)

The other popular term for marriage is to "tie the knot". This phrase is as old as any official recording and is thought to signify the intertwined and permanent nature of marriage, symbolising the strength and unity of two individuals (the ropes) working together to create a new, powerful entity. It since appeared in a number of ways, including small knotted ribbons on dresses. Some believe that it also refers to the strengthening of the wedding bed, in the days when there were no mattresses, and "sleep tight" meant to tighten the ropes that strung across the bed frame.

The term "threshold" is made up of two words "thresh" and "hold". Floors were cold and dry, and only the very rich could afford any form of carpet or rug. Dry straw was put onto the floor, and this was commonly called "thresh". Not only was it warm, it could be collected and thrown out when it was old and dirty. It was also absorbent to the moisture on wet shoes. On top of that, it would have added a fragrance to the otherwise damp and fusty living areas. Because it was loose, it would move around – so the floor was made lower than the doorway, making a small step below the door itself. The job of this step was to "hold" the "thresh" in the room, and gave birth to the term "threshold" meaning the (now mostly) imaginary line across an open doorway. Couples usually went to live in the groom's house, and as the bride would have been unfamiliar with the depths of threshold steps, grooms would carry the bride across the threshold to save her embarrassment at tripping.

WHAT THE DICKENS!
TEACHERS' VERSION

Solution: (Pages: 31-32)

BOZ BONUS CARD 1: Biography

1. **False**: Charles Dickens was christened Charles John Huffam Dickens.
2. **True**: "In adult life he could remember the gaol he had seen in Rochester …and he recalled how he had watched a line of convicts bound together with manacles upon an iron chain."
   Ackroyd, *Dickens* p.51
3. **True**: One of his companions in the factory was Bob Fagin, an orphan.   Ackroyd, *Dickens* p.77
4. **True**: "To keep the clothes of a seventeen year old girl, and to desire to be buried with her, are, even in the context of nineteenth-century enthusiasm, unusual sentiments."
   Ackroyd, *Dickens* p.226
5. **True**: "And in every bar-room and hotel passage the stone passage looks as if it were paved with open oysters."   Ackroyd, *Dickens* p.355
6. **False.**
7. **False.**
8. **True**: He was an actor in a private performance of *The Frozen Deep*, a play he wrote with Wilkie Collins, on 4th July 1857.   Ackroyd, *Dickens* p.785
9. **False**: His last words were "On the ground."   Ackroyd, *Dickens* p.1078
10. **False.**

BOZ BONUS CARD 2: Biography

11. **False.**
12. **True**: "He liked to visit the scenes of murder and to dwell upon the events of the crime itself."
    Ackroyd, *Dickens* p.518
13. **True**: He wrote *The Memoirs of Joseph Grimaldi.*
14. **False.**
15. **False.**
16. **False**: Whilst holidaying in Broadstairs in 1839 he wrote, "got drunk - remarkably drunk - on Tuesday night, was removed by the constables, lay down in front of the house and addressed the multitude for some hours…"   Ackroyd, *Dickens* p.290
17. **True.**
18. **False**: *Jerusalem* was written by William Blake.
19. **False.**
20. **True**:   Ackroyd, *Dickens* p.738-739

BOZ BONUS CARD 3: *Great Expectations*

21. **False.**
22. **False.**
23. **False.**
24. **True.**
25. **False**: It was a filed-through leg iron that was used to attack Mrs. Joe.
26. **True.**
27. **True.**
28. **True.**
29. **False.**
30. **False.**

WHAT THE DICKENS!
TEACHERS' VERSION

Solution: (Pages: 32-33)

BOZ BONUS CARD 4: *Great Expectations*

31. **False.**
32. **True.**
33. **True.**
34. **False:** Matthew Pocket also inherits some, thanks to Pip's intervention.
35. **False.**
36. **True.**
37. **True.**
38. **True.**
39. **False.**
40. **False.**
41. **False.**

BOZ BONUS CARD 5: General Knowledge:

42. **False.**
43. **False.**
44. **False:** He wrote that about *David Copperfield.*
45. **True:** "Phiz" was actually the artist H. K. Browne.
46. **True:** "Charles Dickens visited and revisited the Paris Morgue, lingering there over the faces of the drowned."   Ackroyd, *Dickens* p.519
47. **True:** Visit **http://www.dickensworld.co.uk/media.php** to see and hear the video
48. **False:** It was Alfred Lord Tennyson who wrote that famous poem.
49. **False:** It was called *A Dinner at Poplar Walk.*
50. **True:** He used it to kill off a villain, Krook, in *Bleak House*.
51. **False:** It's an old phrase, meaning "what the devil". Shakespeare used it in *The Merry Wives of Windsor* more than two-hundred years before Charles Dickens was born.
52. **True.**

BOZ BONUS CARD 6: General Knowledge:

53. **True.**
54. **True.** *The Daily Telegraph* 25th June 2008.
55. **False.**
56. **False.**
57. **True:** Ackroyd, *Dickens* p.xii.
58. **False.**
59. **True:** Ackroyd, *Dickens* p.532
60. **True:** Ackroyd, *Dickens* p.xiv

N.B. the references to Ackroyd cited above are taken from Peter Ackroyd's immensely valuable and insightful biography *Dickens*. Guild Publishing 1990 Hardback version (first edition).

WHO ARE YOU?
TEACHERS' VERSION

Solution: (Page: 34)

1	JOE GARGERY	A gentle, caring, blacksmith.	D
2	DOLGE ORLICK	A jealous journeyman worker at the forge.	K
3	HERBERT POCKET	A loyal friend and gentleman.	L
4	COMPEYSON	A deceitful suitor who jilted his bride.	E
5	ABEL MAGWITCH	A transported convict who makes good.	M
6	BENTLEY DRUMMLE	A "blotchy, sulky" aristocrat who seeks wealth.	B
7	WEMMICK	A trusted lawyer's clerk.	G
8	SARAH POCKET	A toady who wants an inheritance.	A
9	MISS HAVISHAM	A wealthy, bitter, recluse who was jilted.	N
10	PHILIP PIRRIP	An orphan boy with a dream.	C
11	ESTELLA	A beautiful girl, trained up for a purpose.	I
12	PUMBLECHOOK	A blustering, pompous, relative of Joe Gargery's.	F
13	CHARLES DICKENS	An author with an amazing tale to tell.	H
14	CLARA BARLEY	A dutiful daughter with an invalided father.	O
15	JAGGERS	A much respected and feared lawyer.	J

8	6	10	1	4	12	7	13	11	15	2	3	5	9	14
A	B	C	D	E	F	G	H	I	J	K	L	M	N	O

WOMEN IN WHITE
TEACHERS' VERSION

Solution: (Page: 35)

Martha Joachim is like Miss Havisham because:

1	She is wealthy.
2	She encountered crime and murder.
3	She broke down due to the actions of her suitor.
4	She became a recluse.
5	She lived in a large house with a walled garden.

AGE SHALL NOT WITHER THEM
TEACHERS' VERSION

Solution: (Page: 36)

Character	Age at beginning	Age when Pip arrives in London	Age in closing sections
Pip	7	18	23
Estella	7	18	23
Herbert	7	18	23
Compeyson	37	48	53
Miss Havisham	40	51	56
Biddy	9-10	19-20	24-25
Joe	29	40	45
Wemmick	34	45	50

The Wisbech manuscript of *Great Expectations* contains papers which show the calculations of age done by Charles Dickens, they are listed above.

QUICK QUOTE QUIZ
TEACHERS' VERSION

Solution: (Page: 40)

Quotation	Character name	Marks available
"Ever the best of friends; aint us, Pip?"	Joe Gargery	1
"Keep still, you little devil, or I'll cut your throat."	Magwitch	1
"You are not afraid of a woman who has never seen the sun since you were born?"	Miss Havisham	1
"You cannot love him Estella!"	Pip	1
"You acted noble, my boy…and I have never forgot it."	Magwitch	1
"If it warn't for me you'd have been to the churchyard long ago, and stayed there. Who brought you up by hand?"	Mrs. Joe (Gargery)	1
"What have I done! What have I done!"	Miss Havisham	1
"…but as to myself, my guiding star always is 'get hold of portable property.' "	Wemmick	3
"On the Rampage, Pip, and off the Rampage, Pip – such is life!"	Joe Gargery	3
"I am instructed to communicate to him, that he will come into a handsome property."	Jaggers	3
"You're a foul shrew, Mother Gargery."	Orlick	3
"He tried to murder me. I should have been a dead man if you had not come up."	Compeyson	3
"My dear Handel, I fear I shall soon have to leave you."	Herbert Pocket	3
"Now…you little coarse monster, what do you think of me now?"	Estella	5
"I was new here once, rum to think of it now!"	Wemmick	5
"Four dogs…and they fought for veal cutlets out of a silver basket."	Pip	5
"And I don't dine, because I'm going to dine at the lady's."	Bentley Drummle	5
"You stock and stone! You cold, cold heart!"	Miss Havisham	5
"…that there hunted dunghill dog wot you kep life in, got his head so high that he could make a gentleman."	Magwitch	5
"I am greatly changed. I wonder you know me."	Estella	5

Possible characters:

Bentley Drummle, Estella, Pip, Miss Havisham, Magwitch, Herbert Pocket, Pumblechook, Compeyson, Wemmick, Mrs. Joe (Gargery), Joe Gargery, Orlick, Jaggers.

GREAT EXPECTATIONS WORD SEARCH
TEACHERS' VERSION

Solution: (Page: 44)

THAT'S NOT MY NAME!

PUMBLECHOOK (1)	JAGGERS (2)	GARGERY (3)	WEMMICK (2)
HAVISHAM (3)	DRUMMLE (3)	POCKET (5)	ORLICK (5)
WOPSLE (1)	COMPEYSON (3)	PIRRIP (2)	TRABB (5)
BIDDY (7)	ESTELLA (3)	HERBERT (4)	BENTLEY (3)

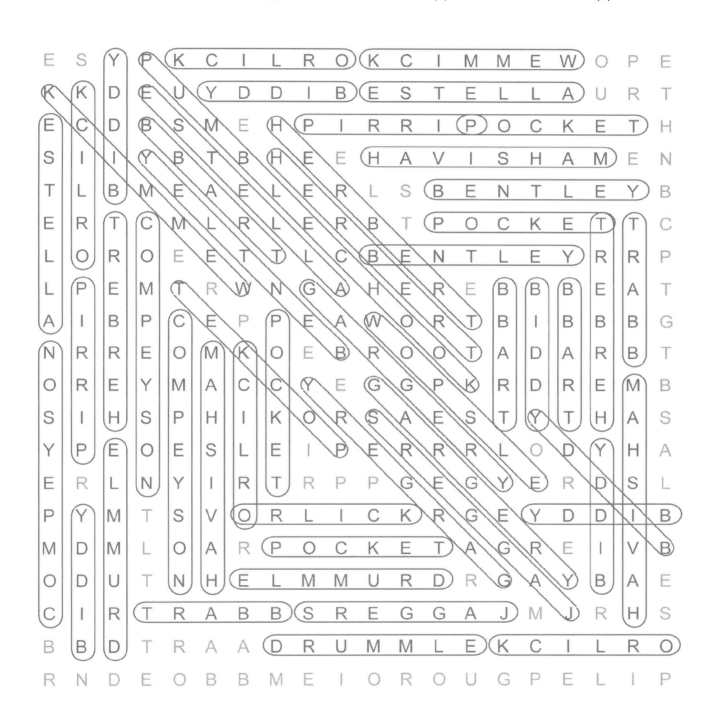

GREAT EXPECTATIONS WORD SEARCH 2
TEACHERS' VERSION

Solution: (Page: 45)

SOMEWHERE MORE FAMILIAR

HULKS (5)　　　　　JOLLY BARGEMEN (5)　　　　BARNARD'S INN (6)
RICHMOND (6)　　　BOTANY BAY (2)　　　　　　THAMES (6)
LITTLE BRITAIN (6)　BLUE BOAR (6)　　　　　　TEMPLE (4)
MARSHES (5)　　　　GRAVESEND (8)　　　　　　LONDON BRIDGE (1)
DENMARK (6)　　　　GREENWICH (8)　　　　　　OLD BATTERY (8)

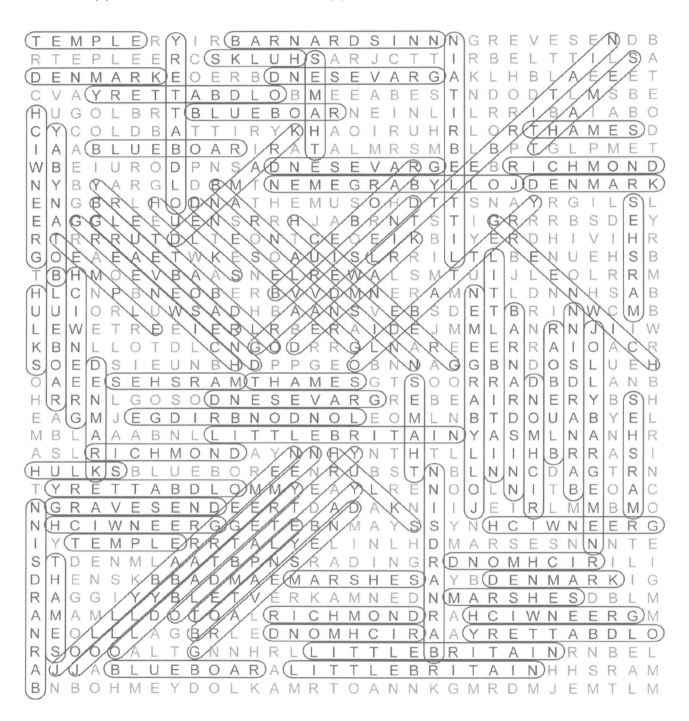

GREAT EXPECTATIONS – CASTIGATE ON EXPERT!
TEACHERS' VERSION

Solution: (Page: 46)

Jumbled spelling	Correct spelling
VISA MISHMASH	MISS HAVISHAM
KEPT BORE RETCH	HERBERT POCKET
TENDERLEY MUMBLE	BENTLEY DRUMMLE
BLOCK UP HOME	PUMBLECHOOK
JOY! RARE EGG	JOE GARGERY
REALLY! A CRAB	CLARA BARLEY
O MY! PONCES	COMPEYSON
OK CHEAP STAR!	SARAH POCKET
GODLIER LOCK	DOLGE ORLICK
HIP! LIP RIP RIP	PHILIP PIRRIP
BE CALM HAG WIT!	ABEL MAGWITCH
LET'S ALE!	ESTELLA
WE MCKIM	WEMMICK
EGGS JAR	JAGGERS
HE'S SLICK DANCER	CHARLES DICKENS

DIGGING DEEPER INTO DIALOGUE
TEACHERS' VERSION

Solution: (Page: 47)

Quote	Character	True meaning
"He calls the knaves, Jacks, this boy!"	Estella	He's a low bred idiot; I'm better than him in every way. I'll make him miserable.
"She brought me up 'by hand'."	Pip	She was not my proper mother, and fed me using a bottle or spoon (although the imagery of the term "by hand" is that she used to hit him instead of care for him)
"…I'm sorry to say, I've eat your pie."	Magwitch	I'll take all of the blame. I won't let any suspicion fall on that dear boy.
"You know best Pip, but don't you think you are happier as you are?"	Biddy	Don't be an idiot Pip! You won't enjoy life trying to be a gentleman. Be happy in your current station in life, with us.
"You and me was ever friends. And when you're well enough to go out for a ride – what larks!"	Joe	I don't care what you've said or done to upset me. I forgive you. When you get better, things between us will be just like they used to be.
"That boy is no common boy, and mark me, his fortun' will be no common fortun'."	Pumblechook	This boy could become wealthy beyond measure and when he does I intend to extract my share!

GARGERISMS: MAY THE FORGE BE WITH YOU!
TEACHERS' VERSION

Solution: (Pages: 48-49)

A	B	C	D	E	F	G	H	I	J	K	L	M	N	O
4	7	8	2	10	3	1	11	5	12	6	9	13	14	15

CHARACTERS AND ADJECTIVES
TEACHERS' VERSION

Solution: (Page: 52)

Pip

ambitious
strong-willed
honest
naive

Estella

vain
confident
dishonest

Joe Gargery

kind
gentle
proud
honest
easy-going

Miss Havisham

scary
intimidating
dishonest
cruel

Abel Magwitch

intimidating
proud
honest
scary

Compeyson

greedy
dishonest

Dolge Orlick

vicious
cruel
scary

Jaggers

cruel
intimidating
intelligent

intelligent	easy-going	kind	weak
proud	independent	intimidating	friendly
strong-willed	immature	timid	vicious
cruel	considerate	greedy	good-humoured
helpful	confident	heroic	honest
dishonest	foolish	scary	naive
gentle	vain	ambitious	kind

WHAT HAPPENS NEXT?
TEACHERS' VERSION

Solution: (Page: 53)

Comic Card	WHAT IS HAPPENING? Describe in your own words. Try to explain what is going on in each panel and what the characters are saying. Can you remember what happens next?
Card 1	The soldiers discover the two convicts, Magwitch and Compeyson, locked in a deadly struggle in the mud. The men are separated by the Sergeant – Compeyson claims that Magwitch was trying to murder him. Magwitch calls him a liar, born and bred. Torches are lit and the convicts are led away. Pip tries to hide his fear as Magwitch gives him a look that "he didn't understand". Magwitch confesses to stealing from the blacksmith, and he and Compeyson are taken back to the hulk.
Card 2	Miss Havisham observes Pip and Estella playing cards. Estella ridicules Pip throughout. Miss Havisham asks Pip what he thinks of Estella. He whispers that she is "very proud...very pretty (and) very insulting". After the game, Estella escorts Pip to the courtyard. She leaves and returns with something for him to eat and drink. She looks contemptuously at him as she leaves. Alone, humiliated and hurt, Pip starts to cry and kicks the wall in frustration. He wanders into the derelict brewery and in the dim interior has a terrifying vision of Miss Havisham hanging by her neck from the beams. When Pip gets home, he lies to his sister and Mr. Pumblechook about his time at Miss Havisham's.
Card 3	Magwitch continues to ask of Pip's fortunes since they met all those years ago on the marshes. Pip starts to shake and almost faints as he realises that his mystery benefactor is, in fact, Magwitch. Pip now realises that Miss Havisham is not his benefactor as he had presumed and, therefore, she has no plans for him and Estella to be together.
Card 4	Pip and Biddy walk along the riverside. Pip is being patronising and blind to the fact that Biddy likes him. He says he is disgusted with his life and that he shall never be happy. He could have settled for a life at the forge, possibly even with Biddy. Instead he is "coarse and common". When Biddy asks who said such a thing, Pip replies "the beautiful young lady at Miss Havisham's" for whom he wants to become a gentleman. Soon after, Pip gets an offer from a mystery benefactor to go to London and become a wealthy gentleman.

GREAT EXPECTATIONS QUIZ
TEACHERS' VERSION

Solution: (Page: 60)

No.	Question	Answer
1	Joe never retaliates when his wife attacks him because: a. He's scared of her b. He's so powerful, he's worried he'd kill her c. He remembers how violent his father was and refuses to act in that way	c
2	Matthew Pocket was turned out of Satis House because: a. He warned Miss Havisham about her fiancé and the financial deals he wanted her to take part in b. He broke every clock in the house c. He told Estella that she had a face like the hind quarters of a cow and ought to try smile at least once each century	a
3	Biddy does not like Orlick because: a. She once saw him beat a stray dog to death with his hammer b. He dares to admire her c. He spends all his time drinking and fighting at the Jolly Bargemen	b
4	At nine o'clock every night Wemmick: a. Takes his "Aged parent" out for a spin in a wheelchair b. Reads about the latest criminal cases at the Old Bailey in his evening paper c. Fires a gun from the top of his "castle"	c
5	Herbert calls Pip by the nickname of Handel because: a. He's so strong he keeps pulling handles off everything in their rooms b. He knows painfully how well Pip can handle himself in a fight c. He likes some music my Handel called *The Harmonious Blacksmith* and thinks that this title fits Pip well	c
6	The Avenger is the name Pip gives to: a. The bull mastiff pup he wins off Drummle in a wager b. The insolent serving boy he hires for himself c. The young man who will tear his insides out, if he does not fetch the convict a file and "wittles"	b

GREAT EXPECTATIONS QUIZ
TEACHERS' VERSION

Solution: (Page: 61)

No.	Question	Answer
7	What nickname does Jaggers give to Bentley Drummle? a. Tickler b. The Spider c. The Red Fox	**b**
8	Pip joins a gentleman's club and becomes a member of: a. The Finches b. The Drones c. The Masons	**a**
9	Herbert Pocket eventually gets a job as: a. A lawyer's clerk b. An estate agent c. A shipping broker	**c**
10	Pip and Herbert first lodge together at: a. Walworth b. Richmond c. Barnard's Inn	**c**
11	Pip discovers that his secret benefactor was: a: Abel Magwitch b: Jaggers c: Miss Havisham	**a**
12	Mrs. Joe was attacked (and some would say murdered) by: a: Joe Gargery b: Compeyson c: Dolge Orlick	**c**
	Mark out of 12:	

READER, I MARRIED HER*
TEACHERS' VERSION

Solution: (Page: 62)

The original ending to *Great Expectations* went as follows:

3.   Drummle's marriage to Estella is a disaster. He uses her cruelly, lives a wild life, and shows no remorse for his actions. A Shropshire doctor, who has seen the outcome of Bentley's violence towards his wife, intercedes on her behalf. Drummle is thrown from his ill treated horse and dies. Estella and the doctor marry. They are poor but happy. When she finally meets Pip again she says that she is greatly changed and pleased to see him. She has now learnt what it is to suffer and understands properly how Pip must have felt.

* The book is *Jane Eyre* by Charlotte Brontë.

FILM VERSIONS
TEACHERS' VERSION

Solution: (Page: 77)

Dreadful name pun number 1: "Jean Simmons shone as the young Estella." Stellar, the Latin root form of Estella, means star. (A star shone…).

Dreadful name pun number 2: "Once you've seen Finlay Currie as Magwitch, you won't be able to picture any other escaping convict inside your head!" (Able –Abel Magwitch).

COMIC PAGE GRID

COMIC SCRIPT - VOLUME 2 CHAPTER 30

Chapter 30

343. The next morning: Pip and Jaggers are breakfasting together at the Blue Boar. Jaggers is looking grimly satisfied, Pip rather alarmed.

Pip vo Top	After considering the matter while dressing at the Blue Boar in the morning, I resolved to tell my guardian that I doubted Orlick's being the right sort of man to fill a post of trust at Miss Havisham's.	I felt it was my duty to warn Mr. Jaggers about Orlick.
Pip		He's not the right sort of man to work for Miss Havisham.
Jaggers	Why of course he's not the right sort of man, Pip, because the man who fills the post of trust never is the right sort of man. Very good, Pip. I'll go round presently, and pay our friend off.	Very good, Pip. I'll dismiss him straight away.
Pip vo Bottom	I was rather alarmed by this summary action.	

344. Pip and Herbert at Barnard's Inn; Herbert has finished his supper of cold meat. A fire burning in the hearth. They are sitting with their feet upon the fender. Herbert has crossed his feet, and is looking at Pip, waiting to hear what he has to say. Pip has laid his hand on Herbert's knee and is earnestly confiding in him.

Pip vo Top	Jaggers and I took the mid-day coach back to London. As soon as I arrived, I went on to Barnard's Inn.	Jaggers and I took the midday coach back to London.
Pip	My dear Herbert, I have something very particular to tell you. Herbert, I love – I adore – Estella.	My dear Herbert, I must tell you something. I love – I adore – Estella.
Herbert	Well? Of course I know that.	I know that!

345. Pip is shocked that Herbert knows

Pip	How do you know it? I never told you.	How?
Herbert	Told me! Why, when you told me your own story, you told me plainly that you began adoring her the first time you saw her.	When you told me your story - you said you adored her from the start.
Pip	I saw her yesterday. And if I adored her before, I now doubly adore her.	If I adored her before, I now doubly adore her.
Herbert	Lucky for you then, if you are picked out and allotted to her.	Lucky for you then, that Miss Havisham is getting you together.

EDUCATIONAL LINKS

USING GRAPHIC NOVELS IN EDUCATION:

The Graphic Classroom

http://graphicclassroom.blogspot.com

> The Graphic Classroom is a resource for teachers and librarians to help them stock high quality, educational-worthy, graphic novels and comics in their classroom or school library. I read and review every graphic novel or comic on this blog and give it a rating as to appropriateness for the classroom.

Graphic Novels for Multiple Literacies

www.readingonline.org/newliteracies/jaal/11-02_column/

> In an increasingly visual culture, literacy educators can profit from the use of graphic novels in the classroom, especially for young adults. Educators need not worry that graphic novels discourage text reading. Lavin (1998) even suggested that reading graphic novels might require more complex cognitive skills than the reading of text alone.

Gretchen E. Schwarz

Graphic Novels across the curriculum

www.ltscotland.org.uk/literacy/images/Graphic%20novels%20across%20the%20curriculum_tcm4-402928.doc

Mel Gibson

PROMOTING LITERACY IN THE CLASSROOM:

NATE – National Association for the Teaching of English

www.nate.org.uk/

> A national voice on key issues affecting English teaching. NATE is also an active member of the International Federation of the Teachers of English where it seeks to share the experience of English teachers in the UK and learn from teachers in diverse parts of the world.

Graphic novels – engaging readers and encouraging literacy

www.ltscotland.org.uk/literacy/findresources/graphicnovels/index.asp

> The showcase resource highlights how graphic novels can be used throughout the curriculum.

Learning and Teaching Scotland

Reviews, news, opinion, awards, newsletters

www.teensreadtoo.com/

> Books for teens, encouraging literacy.

Two teachers... who read... a lot!

http://readingyear.blogspot.com/2008/03/shakespeare-for-all.html

> Franki and Mary write, read, review.

Expanding Literacies through Graphic Novels

www1.ncte.org/Library/files/Free/recruitment/EJ0956Expanding.pdf

> Gretchen Schwarz offers a rationale, based on the need for current students to learn multiple literacies, for the use of graphic novels in the high school English class. She highlights several titles, suggests possible classroom strategies, and discusses some of the obstacles teachers may face in adding graphic novels to their curriculum.

Gretchen E. Schwarz

Eek! Comics in the Classroom!

www.education-world.com/a_curr/profdev/profdev105.shtml

> More and more teachers are finding that once-maligned comics, and their big brothers graphic novels, can be effective tools for teaching a multitude of literacy skills to students with a variety of learning needs.

Education World

EDUCATIONAL LINKS

UKLA
United Kingdom Literacy Association
www.ukla.org/

> The United Kingdom Literacy Association (UKLA) is a registered charity, which has as its sole objective the advancement of education in literacy. UKLA is concerned with literacy education in school and out-of-school settings in all phases of education and members include classroom teachers, teaching assistants, school literacy co-ordinators, LEA literacy consultants, teacher educators, researchers, inspectors, advisors, publishers and librarians.

Using Comics and Graphic Novels in the Classroom
engres.ied.edu.hk/lang_arts/onlineRead/comics/NCTEUsingComicsNGraphicNovelsIntheClassrm.pdf

> Educators also see the educational potential of comics and graphic novels. They can help with building complex reading skills, according to Shelley Hong Xu, associate professor in the department of teacher education at California State University, Long Beach. She says that graphic novels and comics should have a classroom role similar to other children's literature.

The National Council of Teachers of English (NCTE)

Teen Librarian
www.teenlibrarian.co.uk/

> Reviews, news, games and books.

Have fun, get creative...
www.getemreading.com/

> "Nothing compares to the feeling I get when I help a student discover the magic of reading. My experiences have taught me that it is never too late to turn a non-reader into a reader –
> IT JUST TAKES THE RIGHT BOOK!"

Getting graphic! Using graphic novels to promote literacy with pre teens and teens
http://findarticles.com/p/articles/mi_m0PBX/is_4_38/ai_n6123048

> Getting Graphic! also tackles the big question: are graphic novels, aka comic books, "junk literature for children," or do they have a "cultural and educational value and belong on the shelves of libraries across the nation"?

Michele Gorman

MAKING COMICS AND GRAPHIC NOVELS:-

National Association of Comic Art Educators
www.teachingcomics.org/

> One of the primary goals of NACAE is to assist educational institutions and individual educators interested in establishing a comics art curriculum. Excellent links, and papers on the topic of Comics in the Classroom.

NACAE

ROK Comics
www.rokcomics.com/comiccreator.html

> The new way to deliver comics to mobile phones. Use the FREE FOR ALL OPTION to:
> • Publish strips for free
> • Create embed samples for your website or blog
> • Have fun!

Comic Life
www.rm.com/shops/rmshop/Product.aspx?cref=PD1140288

> Lets you create comics, beautiful picture albums, how-to's... and more!
> Can be used on whiteboards with electronic copies of the books in this series.

EDUCATIONAL LINKS

GENERAL GRAPHIC NOVEL SITES:-

Graphic Novel Review Site for Teens

www.noflyingnotights.com

> Covers everything from superheroes to historical novels via manga and cartoons.
>
> **Robin Brenner**

Comics Worth Reading

http://comicsworthreading.com

> Independent Opinions by Johanna Draper Carlson and friends
> News and reviews of graphic novels, manga, comic books, and related subjects.

Comic Shop Voice

www.comicshopvoice.co.uk/

> UK site with articles, news, reviews and comic events.

Forbidden Planet

http://forbiddenplanet.co.uk

> International blog of all things comic.

DICKENS RELATED SITES AND ORGANISATIONS:-

BBC

www.bbc.co.uk/schools/gcsebitesize/english_literature/prosegreatexpect/

> Contains a variety of interactive resources and tests to help school pupils working on *Great Expectations*

www.bbc.co.uk/arts/multimedia/dickens/index_popup.shtml

> A cleverly constructed BBC Arts interactive game poses the questions: could you survive in Dickens's London? Dare you take a tour of Dickensian London? You could meet Mr. Micawber, Mr. Pickwick or Fagin? Or you might catch smallpox and end up in jail? If you do well, you'll get to meet Charles Dickens. Be warned; time is short and the streets of London are not for the faint hearted...

www.bbc.co.uk/drama/bleakhouse/animation.shtml

> Lets you see a fabulous animated biography of the writer.
> (This could be shown to pupils prior to playing WHAT THE DICKENS! on page 30)

Charles Dickens

http://charlesdickenspage.com/index.html

> David Perdue's award-winning website on Charles Dickens is a must for its wealth of links and resources. The Dickens London map could prove to be invaluable for pupils attempting to research and create their own map of Magwitch's flight.

www.helsinki.fi/kasv/nokol/dickens.html

> Dickens's life and works.

Dickens World

www.dickensworld.co.uk

> Worth visiting for the Dickens timeline alone, this website has several interactive resources and ideas for teachers and pupils. Make sure you see The Hoosiers video!

About Charles Dickens

www.underthesun.cc/Classics/Dickens/

> His works, resources, and timeline.

EDUCATIONAL LINKS / PLACES TO VISIT

Poverty and families in the Victorian Era

www.hiddenlives.org.uk/articles/poverty.html

> This article by Barbara Daniels gives an overview of the causes and effects of poverty on poor families and children in Victorian Britain. At the time of writing, Barbara is a Ph.D. student with the Department of Religious Studies, at The Open University. Her subject is "Street Children and Philanthropy in the latter half of the 19th Century".

Charles Dickens – Gads Hill Place

www.perryweb.com/Dickens/life_main.shtml

> His life, works, family, career and friends.

A Dickens Chronology

www.lang.nagoya-u.ac.jp/~matsuoka/CD-Chro.html

> Excellent, comprehensive site.

The Victorian Web

www.victorianweb.org/authors/dickens/index.html

> His works, social history, political history, images, and themes.

Life in Victorian England

www.aboutbritain.com/articles/life-in-victorian-england.asp

> Inventions, clothes, houses, toys, schools and society.

THE LANDSCAPES OF *GREAT EXPECTATIONS:-*

The Hoo Peninsular, Kent

> The Hoo Peninsular is a marshland area lying between the estuaries of the rivers Thames and Medway. These are the marshes of *Great Expectations*, and is where the prison ships (the "hulks") were moored. Walking is the only way to properly access this area and sample the atmosphere. Fortunately, The Saxon Shore Way, a long distance coastal path, tracks around some of the main byways. The villages of Cliffe, and Cooling should not be missed. The ruined battery at Cliffe Creek, guarding the mouth of the river, might have suggested to Dickens the "Old Battery" where Pip met Magwitch.

St. James Church, Cooling, Kent

> Situated 6 miles north of Rochester, off the B2000, lies a 13th century church that Dickens knew well and which inspired the opening of *Great Expectations*. Step into the graveyard and you'll be in the real landscape where Magwitch grabbed Pip. Look towards the Church door and you'll see the amazing stone tablet graves he describes in the opening paragraphs; they are known as "Pip's graves" locally.

Rochester, Kent

> The "market town" where Pumblechook trades and Satis House is located, is taken to be Rochester. Mention is made of the Cathedral chimes in Chapter 49. Dickens lived close by at Gads Hill Place. Rochester was often mentioned in his writings, particularly in his last, unfinished, novel *The Mystery of Edwin Drood*.

Restoration House

17-19 Crow Lane, Rochester, Kent. ME1 1RF

> Said to be the building that fired Dickens's imagination to create the dark, decaying, nightmarish, Satis House, Restoration House has recently undergone extensive renovations and is now open to the public for viewing.

PLACES TO VISIT

The Forge
Forge Lane, Chalk, Kent

In 1836, Dickens and his wife Catherine honeymooned for a week in the village of Chalk, near Gravesend. Although many of the older buildings have now been destroyed, the old forge, which is understood to have been the model for Joe Gargery's forge in *Great Expectations*, still stands and can be seen from outside. It is a private residence. (No tours!).

Other places of interest:

The Charles Dickens Museum
48 Doughty Street, London, WC1N 2LX

The writer lived here from 1837-1839. The museum contains restored rooms and furniture, letters, pictures, memorabilia and some first editions.

The Guildhall Museum
High Street, Rochester, Kent

This museum features a full size reconstruction of part of a Medway prison hulk and a "Dickens Discovery Room." Admission is free.

Charles Dickens Birthplace Museum
393 Old Commercial Road, Portsmouth, Hampshire, England, PO1 4QL

This location allows you the chance to visit the place where Charles Dickens was born. The house has been restored and decorated to give it a Regency feel. Teacher packs are available.

Dickens House Museum
2 Victoria Parade, Broadstairs, Kent, CT10 1QS

Charles Dickens was a regular holidaymaker to this house, overlooking the sands and the sea. The owner of the house supposedly reported to Dickens that she had the right to chase donkeys off the lawn at the front of the house!

Dickens World
Leviathan Way, Chatham Maritime, Kent, ME4 4LL

This amazing place has the layout and feel of a Dickensian theme park, or stage settings from a high quality film production, but is far more educational than that. It features a variety of attractions for the family, live performances of some of Dickens's works, an animatronics presentation, a *Great Expectations* boat ride, where you sneak through London's watery back ways, a 4D cinema show at Pegotty's boathouse about Charles Dickens, a haunted house and a wealth of curios and entertainments.

DICKENS FESTIVALS:-

During the first weekend in June, since 1978, the city of Rochester has hosted its highly popular Dickens Festival. Each day, a parade of characters, dressed in appropriate costumes, march through the streets of the city. There are music, dance, drama and street theatre events. Thousands now visit and enjoy this summer festival. A Christmas festival, incorporating many Dickensian elements, also takes place in December.

For more details on these events visit the Medway City Council website at:
www.medway.gov.uk/index/leisure/events/dickensfestival.htm

Broadstairs, on the East Kent coast, also stages an annual Dickens Festival in the summer. This was where Dickens and his family holidayed for many years, and some of his favourite books were written overlooking the bay. In 2008, a wide variety of Dickens themed events were staged between the 19th and the 22nd June.

www.broadstairsdickensfestival.co.uk/

GREAT EXPECTATIONS: ON AUDIO

A BBC Radio dramatisation featuring Douglas Hodge and Geraldine McEwan together with a full cast is available from BBC Audio books.
ISBN: 978-0-563406-92-1

A freely downloadable audio version of the book, suitable for playing on MP3, can be found courtesy of Project Gutenberg at:
www.gutenberg.org/etext/8608

Penguin Classics and Brilliance Audio have produced an MP3/CD unabridged version, narrated by Michael Page.
ISBN: 978-1-593351-59-5

In addition to this, Penguin Classics also have a version read by Hugh Laurie.
ISBN: 978-0-140620-16-0

Martin Jarvis has narrated a version for CSA Word.
ISBN: 978-1-901768-38-1

A free extract of Martin Jarvis reading the novel can be found at:
http://odeo.com/episodes/22590629-GREAT-EXPECTATIONS-by-Charles-Dickens-Read-by-Martin-Jarvis

An abridged version, produced by Naxos, featuring Anton Lesser as narrator, is available in a variety of formats.
ISBN: 978-9-626340-82-0

An educational study guide version featuring Jonathan Lomas, and produced by Smartpass Limited, can also be obtained.
ISBN: 978-1-903362-11-2

Great Expectations -The Musical
www.greatexpectationsmusical.com/music.html
    Hear extracts from the songs in a musical version of the novel.